BEHIND THE HOME BAR

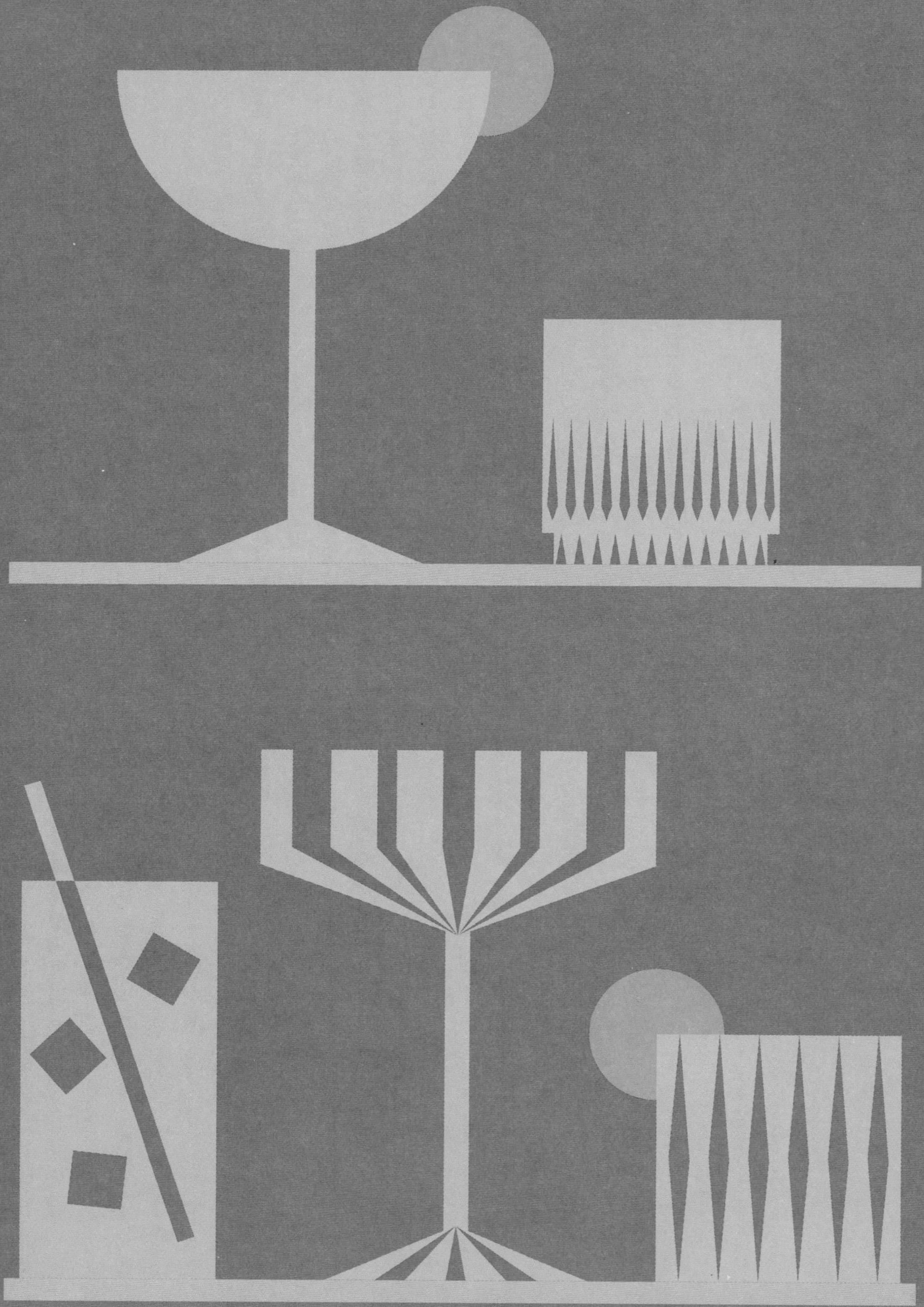

BEHIND THE HOME BAR

CARA DEVINE

**The essential
guide to making
cocktails at home**

Hardie Grant

BOOKS

CONTENTS

WHY DO YOU NEED THIS BOOK?

Even the most dedicated of home bartenders can get stuck in a rut sometimes. Unless you're willing to spend your pay cheque on a host of new bottles every month, it can feel difficult to get creative. So, I want to introduce you to some secrets of the trade to help make the most of your home bar set-up. I'll also teach you how to layer fun flavours into drinks so you don't get bored and can continue to delight yourself and your guests come cocktail hour!

My name is Cara Devine and I have been a cocktail bartender for almost fifteen years. What drew me to this industry was being able to make someone's day a little bit better; to participate in that moment when a person sits at the bar, has a chat, orders a drink and you see their stresses and strains start to melt away. Whether you make them a great version of an old favourite or surprise them with a new flavour combination, the aim is to please – and that's a noble aim. Having spent many years behind the bar, I decided to share my love and knowledge of drinks through my YouTube channel, Behind the Bar with Cara Devine. This has helped me connect with lots of passionate bartenders, both expert and amateur, and get a better understanding of the challenges that face those wanting to whip up professional-standard cocktails at home.

While there is an undeniable charm about sitting at the bar of a consummate hospitality professional, there's no reason that you can't recreate that same magic in your own home (you will have to do your own dishes though, unfortunately). You may not have access to the same range of bottles as your local cocktail bar, but with a well-stocked pantry, some good fresh produce and a few key techniques under your belt, you will have an array of incredible flavours at your disposal to zhuzh the couple of bottles you do have.

You needn't throw the kitchen sink at it either; classic cocktails are classics for a reason – they are delicious and well-balanced with just a few simple ingredients. Thinking about how you can switch out ingredients for other complementary flavours in a tried-and-tested recipe is one of the easiest ways to start your own creative process.

My first book, *Strong, Sweet and Bitter*, explored how these three pillars of flavour (strong, sweet, and bitter or sour) underpin every well-balanced drink. I call this the 'Taste Triangle'. I broke down well-known cocktails into their constituent parts to show what each ingredient brings to the party, and empowered readers to make substitutions according to their own taste. An obvious

example of this is the Negroni: a three-equal-parts cocktail where gin constitutes the strong base, vermouth adds sweetness and Campari brings bitterness to create a harmonious symphony of flavour. But you can switch each of these ingredients for something that plays the same role. For example, in the East India Negroni, rum replaces the gin and cream sherry the vermouth for a richer, more dessert-style take which still hits each point of the Taste Triangle.

In this book I want to take this idea even further by showing you how you can apply this same creative approach in the comfort of your own home. You can make or customise ingredients to add your own flair to bespoke recipes. Sure, bars have fancy-pants technology that they can use for their home-made ingredients, but you'd be amazed at how much you can achieve with just a saucepan and a sieve! Using the preservation techniques detailed in this book – many of which have been around for centuries – just one trip to the market can stock your fridge, freezer and pantry with an array of flavours that will delight your palate.

So, I'll lead you through how to get prepped for success, starting with your home bar set-up. Think of it like a capsule wardrobe:

you don't have to have one of everything, but you do want to make sure that every bottle is a versatile heavy hitter. Similarly, you don't have to have every fancy bar or kitchen tool, but some key equipment will help you level up exponentially. Finally, you drink with your eyes first, so we'll look at some accessible glassware and garnishes to make the drinking experience five star.

Once we've got everything set up, we'll look at some winning 'Flavour friends'; having an arsenal of trusted combinations can give you confidence when you want to whip something new up on the fly. Using the charts on pages 52–55 can help you decide which of the prep and cocktail recipes you want to try. These make up the rest of the book and will cover all sorts of tips, tricks and techniques to give your drinks the wow factor.

Ultimately, if you love delicious drinks and want to know how to create them for you and your guests at home, this is the book for you. So, let's get mixing!

SETTING UP YOUR HOME BAR

It can seem a bit daunting to level up from mixing yourself the odd Martini or Old Fashioned at the end of the day to preparing home-made shrubs and sherbets, but using rotovaps and sous-vide machines isn't the only way to pack your drinks with flavourful ingredients. You'll find that you already have many common pieces of equipment to hand, perhaps just on a smaller scale.

Getting both your bar area (whether that's a shelf, trolley or corner of the kitchen bench) and kitchen organised takes a lot of the stress out of making drinks, especially if you're entertaining. Use this section to decide what is important to you, and if there is anything you need to invest in to make your life easier.

MISE EN PLACE

/miz ɑ̃ ˈplas/

noun (French)

the gathering and preliminary preparation of the
ingredients and equipment to be used in cooking
or serving food ... or, in this case, drinks!

STOCKING YOUR 'BACK BAR'

NOTE

Any one of the categories in this section could fill a book themselves (and most have!), but here I'm going to focus more on different styles within each category, and how to choose what you should buy based on what you want to use it for. (And, what to look for – and ignore! – on the label.) If you would like more information on anything specific, I have lots of deep dives and discussion of specific brands on my YouTube channel which complement the information here.

Of course, it's great to have a well-stocked bar, but you don't need to have one of every bottle under the sun to start mixing up a storm at home. So, what do you *really* need?

The main thing to remember is that this is YOUR bar – sure, you might want to keep a bottle of your mother-in-law's favourite tipple on hand for brownie points, but I suggest tailoring your selection to your unique taste. If gin is your drink of choice, for instance, it makes more sense to invest in a few different gins with varied flavour profiles and have fun with those instead of having lots of different spirits. Similarly, if you can't stand aniseed (okay, I might be projecting here – it's my nemesis) then give the pastis and absinthe a miss; there are plenty of other ways to add an herbal element to drinks.

Don't forget there are loads of recipes in this book to help customise ingredients, too, so if you buy a bottle you're not such a fan of, it's no problem. You can simply transform it into an infusion or a home-made liqueur instead!

SPIRITS

Spirits are often the star of a cocktail, but they're also usually the biggest investment, so it pays to be tactical about what you buy. Expensive doesn't always mean better; a lot of those 'premium' big-name brands have a large marketing budget behind them, which is reflected in their price *wink wink*. If you can, try seeking out local distillers, as buying direct is not only budget friendly but you get to support smaller businesses at the same time. That said, well-known brands have solid consistency and are more widely available so might make more sense for you.

Taste as widely as you can. If you're at a bar with a large range of spirits, take a chance and try something different. You may well find a new favourite! Consider what style of drink you're most likely to make as well. If you prefer fruity, tropical cocktails, for example, then a solid, work-house spirit – like a classic London Dry gin – that won't break the bank makes more sense to buy as it can be easily mixed with lots of other flavours. If you gravitate towards spirit-forward drinks like the Old Fashioned, it's perhaps worth splurging on something a little more special as it will be the main focus and stand-out flavour.

ALCOHOL BY VOLUME (ABV)

A spirit is a substance that has been distilled: the process of separating water from alcohol and other substances, which concentrates the alcohol. This means it has a much higher ABV than substances like beer and wine, which have been fermented to produce alcohol, but not distilled. There are some rules around minimum alcohol concentration. Scotch, for example, has to be at least 40 per cent ABV to be labelled as Scotch, but these rules vary from category to category and country to country. Less than 40 per cent ABV can be an indicator of cost-cutting on the part of the producer as they have tried to 'stretch' their spirit by diluting it (although this is not a hard-and-fast rule). That said, a higher ABV doesn't necessarily mean better – yes, that cask-strength whisky at 60 per cent ABV may well be delicious, but serving your guests double-shot cocktails with it will probably result in some casualties! I find 40–46 per cent ABV to be the sweet spot for mixing.

Vodka

Vodka does, undeniably, lean towards the neutral end of spirits, but it is extremely versatile and there are some stylistic variations between brands. The flavour is most heavily influenced by what it is made from. For example, a lot of vodkas are made from wheat, and should be smooth and slightly sweet. In ones made from rye, you might detect a hint of spice, and potato vodkas are generally earthier and more textural – ideal for a dirty Martini. For most vodka drinks you just want a well-made product, i.e. one that doesn't taste harsh, which will provide a crisp and clean backbone to your drinks.

Vodka also makes a good blank canvas for infusions and tinctures. For these, a higher alcohol content will help draw out more flavour, so finding something 40 per cent ABV or above will produce the best results. Of course, you can buy flavoured vodkas as well, but try to find ones that use natural ingredients rather than synthetic, as less-pleasant artificial flavours can quickly take a cocktail from hero to zero!

What to look for

First and foremost, be sure what your vodka is made from. Also, be sure not to get sucked in by how many times it has been distilled; most vodkas are distilled on a column still, and marketers can be a little sneaky and count each plate within the still as a 'distillation'. All vodka is highly rectified, so unless you're drinking something your neighbour distilled in their shed it should be a clean spirit.

Gin

While gin, by definition, has to contain juniper – the berries that provide gin's distinctive citrus and pine notes – the rest is really up to interpretation. Classic London Dry gins will lean more heavily on the juniper profile, usually with just a few other botanicals to support. Good examples of these are punchy and bright with a nice oily texture, and they work excellently in most classic cocktail formats, especially ones that hero the spirit.

The 'contemporary' gin trend sought to bring more people on the gin train, pulling back on the juniper for a lighter, more floral flavour profile that is crowd pleasing (a well-known brand usually served with cucumber is a good example). This style works well in light and fresh drinks, and can easily be substituted for vodka to add an extra dimension.

Nowadays, the world is gin's oyster. Quite literally, in fact; I've even had an oyster shell gin! Distilleries often utilise regional botanicals to give their gins an X-factor, so whether you love a big citrus bomb, something spicy and warm, or want to take a walk on the savoury side, there's a gin for you. It also means that any gin cocktail can be given a whole new persona depending on the bottle you reach for – try a simple Sour with a few different gins and see how much it changes.

What to look for

The main thing to pay attention to with gin is its key botanicals, as this can help you figure out your likes and dislikes. Personally, I like savoury gins so look for ones with maritime herbs, but I tend to stay away from anything too floral as I find them a little soapy. You might be the opposite.

Agave spirits

Tequila has absolutely exploded in recent years and with it has come a new interest in agave spirits in general.

Tequila itself is heavily regulated. It has to be made in Mexico, mostly in Jalisco around the town of Tequila, and another couple of municipalities. It also has to be made from blue weber agave specifically. It can be unaged (blanco) or aged (reposado, añejo, extra añejo and so on). Because of this it is extremely versatile; grassy and fruity blancos make ideal substitutes for vodka, gin and white rums, and aged tequilas can provide delicious twists on whisk(e)y or dark rum cocktails.

Mezcal is a much broader category – think of it like wine. It can be made in lots of different regions and from many different agaves, and all of these influences will have an effect on the flavour outcome. It's regularly said that mezcal is smoky, but that's not necessarily true. For mezcal, the agave hearts (or piñas) are often baked underground with charcoal, as opposed to baking or steaming as is usual for tequila, and this is what can impart a smoky flavour. However, not all mezcals are smoky. It's honestly one of the most diverse spirit categories I've ever tried, so tasting widely is recommended. I often get notes of jalapeño, pepper and tropical fruits, but I tell you one thing – I've never been bored by a mezcal.

If you're an avid agave admirer, keep going. There is sotol, raicilla and even Australian or Californian agave to explore. The big thing to bear in mind is that this kind of spirit is not easy to produce – and that comes with a (well-earned) price tag.

What to look for

For tequila, it must be made from 100 per cent blue weber agave. 'Mixto', i.e. tequila that has up to 49 per cent other stuff added to it, is what gave you a headache when you were younger. For mezcal, look for 'ancestral' (made with ancient methods) or 'artisanal' (where some modern updates are allowed, but they're generally sticking to a traditional way of making it). Don't be scared of 'destilados de agave'. This is often used as a way of signifying that the producer does things properly but just doesn't want to go through the paperwork and somewhat arbitrary standards to have their tequila or mezcal certified.

Sugarcane spirits

WTF is a sugarcane spirit? Well, rum, of course! But also some other well-known spirit categories like cachaça. Using the broader term is especially important in countries like Australia, where rum has to be aged for at least two years to legally be called 'rum', but spirits are being produced which are similar to rum agricoles (made from fresh sugarcane juice instead of molasses), or just younger rums (not aged for the requisite amount of time). These will be labelled as 'cane spirits' even though they would be called rum if made elsewhere.

There is a huge variety of production methods in this category, and so it is a much more versatile spirit than you might think. Don't limit it to tropical drinks (as delicious as they may be). Sugarcane spirits can be substituted into most cocktail recipes you can think of. I love a rum Old Fashioned made with a funky pot-still rum, or an El Presidente – essentially a Cuban Manhattan – with an elegant, lighter style. Of course, spiced rums are a fun way to layer other flavours into cocktails, but be wary of their sweetness level; you may need to pull back on other sweet ingredients to keep the drink balanced.

What to look for

Rum is a notoriously badly labelled genre, as every country that produces it has different rules, so it's hard to put classifications on it. Just don't be drawn in by the colour of the liquid; 'white rum' can actually be aged and filtered, and caramel colouring can be used to make a rum darker. When it comes to age labelling, rum has nothing like the conventions of Scotch, for example. In many rum-producing countries, they can put the age of the oldest rum in the blend on the bottle, but the majority of the liquid is actually younger. 'Rum agricole' will be less heavy and more herbal so can be substituted for lighter spirits like vodka and gin, whereas molasses rum is chewier and fuller-bodied, so can be substituted for darker spirits like whisk(e)y.

Brandy

When we think of the most 'elite' spirits in the world, brandy – Cognac and Armagnac – often springs to mind. You might think that you're not fancy enough to have tried brandy, but I bet you've had a pisco sour? If so, you've had brandy! Brandy is just any spirit made from distilling a fruit-based wine. It comes from the Dutch word *brandewijn*, which literally means burnt wine.

Grape brandy is common, but you can also make brandy from apples, pears, peaches, cherries, etc. Essentially, if you can ferment it, you can make brandy from it. This makes it a really fun ingredient to play with in cocktails. I love substituting it into whisk(e)y-based drinks for a fruitier, richer experience.

What to look for

Grape brandy can just be labelled 'brandy', while anything made from other fruits will say so on the label. Certain regions have specific labelling practices – in Cognac, for instance, VS denotes a brandy aged for at least two years; VSOP is at least four years old, and XO at least ten years old. This is copied by some other brandies of the same style around the world. However, older isn't always better; I actually like using a young and fresh VS for cocktails as the older, oakier styles can be harder to balance. You can also use unaged brandies like pisco and grappa for a fun twist on vodka or gin drinks.

Whisk(e)y

As singer-songwriter John Lee Hooker sang, 'one Scotch, one bourbon, one beer' ... sounds like a strong order to me! I don't like to discriminate and love all styles of whisk(e)y. With the boom in whisk(e)y, we've seen a lot of innovation and traditional geographical distinctions thrown out of the window; single malts are being made in the US and rye whiskies in Scotland, while countries like Australia and India have become major players. I've tried world blends, whisky fermented with sake yeast and whiskey finished in absinthe barrels, so if whisk(e)y is your jam, do some research as there's plenty of room for experimentation!

That said, for cocktail making, a solid bourbon, rye whiskey and blended Scotch-style whisky will stand you in good stead. You don't have to splurge (although if you want to, go ahead). But something decent quality and ideally a slightly higher ABV – around 45 per cent – will mix well.

What to look for

Bourbon is at least 51 per cent corn, making it generally rounder and sweeter. What the other 49 per cent is made up of will have a big impact – if it has a high rye content, it will be spicier, whereas wheat will make it softer and smoother. Rye is at least 51 per cent rye – think of rye bread; the higher the rye content the drier and spicier it will be. Single malt is 100 per cent malted barley from a single distillery, and every distillery will have a distinctive flavour profile due to production choices, such as whether to use peat, the shape of the still and what barrels are used to age the whisky. These whiskies can be a little harder to balance in drinks, especially if they are heavily peated, but they can also make spectacular sippers in the right recipe. Blended whiskies, which are a blend of malt and lighter-grain whisky, are generally a little easier to work with – and a little easier on the bank balance!

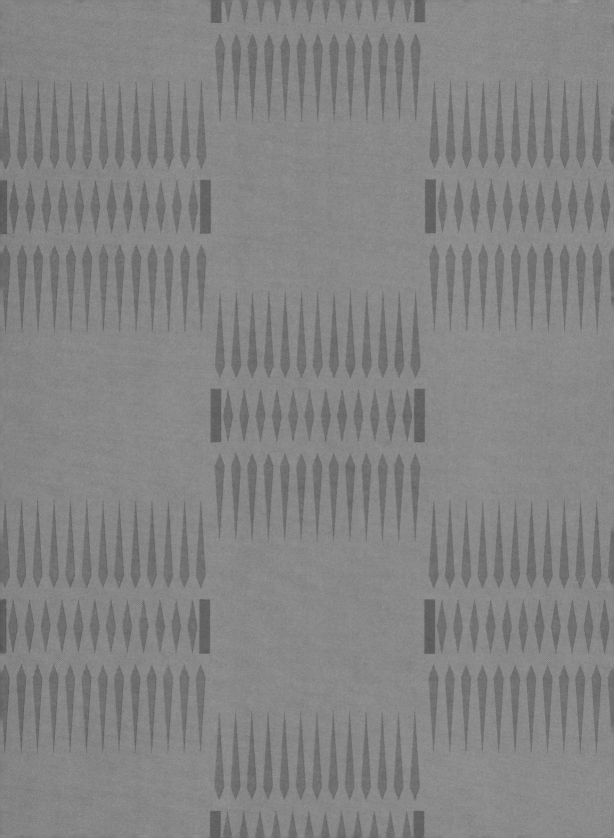

NOT SPIRITS

Often known as modifiers, your 'not spirits' can be the key to diversification in your cocktail making. They're generally cheaper than spirits and having a range can allow you to use one bottle of spirit in lots of different ways. As with spirits, these can be personalised through infusions (see page 102), and some are definitely complex enough to form the base of a cocktail by themselves.

Liqueurs

Let's face it: everybody loves a sweet treat and cocktails do need some sugar for balance. Liqueurs can be an excellent way to introduce this, with a little extra panache! Liqueurs are a broad church; they have a spirit base and are sweetened but, beyond that, they come in all flavours under the sun. Again, personal preference should be your main guide here; if you don't like coffee then don't bother buying a coffee liqueur!

Generally speaking, one citrus liqueur (orange is the most common, either triple sec or curaçao), one berry (blackcurrant, blackberry or raspberry, often known as their French translations cassis, mûre and framboise) and one more dessert style (crème de cacao, amaretto, coffee) will do the trick. There is also a joke that elderflower liqueur is a bartender's band-aid; its floral sweetness will lift almost any cocktail.

What to look for

Be wary of anything too brightly coloured. Most brands that use natural flavourings and colourings over synthetic alternatives will boast about it, and it tastes much better.

Fortified wines

Probably my favourite of the modifiers, there is hardly a cocktail that can't be improved by a fortified wine, in my opinion! This covers everything from vermouth to port to sherry (both sweet, off-dry and dry) to sake – anything that is wine based but fortified with more alcohol. Some are also flavoured with botanicals.

There is an amazing complexity to these wines, generally at an excellent price point, too. Of course, you can't make a Martini without vermouth, but try a splash in a tropical cocktail for an herbal boost. Dry sherry, such as fino or manzanilla, can bring a dry and saline edge to citrusy drinks, while port and madeira add a wonderful richness to nightcaps.

For most, one dry and one sweeter example of these wines will cover your bases. 'Aromatised' wines and vermouth will also add botanical elements of herbs, citrus and some bitterness, whereas straight fortifieds like sherry, port and madeira will have more of a wine presence. Just remember that because they are wine based they don't last forever, so keep them in the fridge once opened and taste before using if they've been open for a while. If they don't taste as good anymore, no stress – use them for cooking!

What to look for

Each of the styles within these categories have their own labelling conventions. Have a look at my YouTube channel for a deeper explanation of each. Try looking for local examples using native botanicals to add some unexpected flavour elements. If you're worried about moving through them before they go off, some brands do smaller 350 ml (12 oz) or 500 ml (17 oz) bottles which is very handy.

Amari

Bitter isn't always bad! This broad category of herbal liqueurs adds depth and interest like no other. These are multifaceted ingredients – they have a pronounced bitterness, of course, but they also have sugar added for balance and body, and each example has its own botanical profile. Some are more citrus led, while others are more floral or savoury.

Due to this complexity, they can form the base of a cocktail – like in a Spritz – or add an intriguing accent to other types of drinks. It's handy to have a couple of different styles on hand: one brighter, more citrusy/juicy option and one more savoury and herbal will suffice for most recipes.

What to look for

The main botanicals will give you an idea of the flavour profile of each amaro. Try using the flavour pairing section of this book to come up with some interesting combinations.

Cocktail bitters and tinctures

These are the seasonings of the bar world. Cocktail missing a little somethin' somethin'? Might need a dash or two of bitters, or a tincture. Both are strongly flavoured infusions used in small quantities. The difference is in the name; bitters always contain a bittering agent, like wormwood or gentian, whereas tinctures don't. Both, however, provide extra dimension and length to a drink.

Most classic recipes call for the kind of bitters that were used for medicinal purposes – intensely herbal, woody and spicy. You should definitely have one of this style on hand, but also have some fun with them. The range available nowadays means you can tailor them to match your favourite spirits and the type of cocktails you like to make. I love a locally made grapefruit and agave bitters in my Margaritas, for example, or their cacao and macadamia version in an Old Fashioned. And, of course, you can also make your own – see pages 118 and 119.

What to look for

Again, the flavourings here are the most important thing. Be aware that bitters are generally alcoholic, but are used in such small measures that they hardly raise the overall ABV of the drink (bearing in mind that anything up to 0.5 per cent ABV is legally non-alcoholic; even some food products have tiny percentages of alcohol in them). However, there are now some non-alcoholic bitters on the market if you are concerned when using them in non-alcoholic drinks.

THE PANTRY

Once the booze is bought, it's time to think about your pantry. As with cooking, having some shelf-stable ingredients on hand when mixing drinks will give you added flair on the fly! If, like me, you're not one to plan ahead, these can be lifesavers in a pinch.

SWEET TREATS

Let's start with the basics. Every cocktail contains sweetness in some form, and without it the drink will be thin and unbalanced, so don't be scared of it!

Sugar

Some regular white granulated sugar will stand you in good stead to make anything from simple sugar syrup (see page 65) to flavoured syrups like vanilla, cinnamon or fruit syrups. You can also bring extra flavour by using a more intense brown sugar like demerara or muscovado, which work particularly well with darker spirits.

Honey/Maple syrup/Agave nectar

Easy substitutes (if you can't even be bothered making sugar syrup; see page 65) are nature's syrups: honey, maple or agave. Almost any spirit tastes great just shaken up with lemon and one of these. You can experiment with different ones as well – some are lighter and more floral, others can be earthier and more herbal. You can infuse them, too (see page 77). It can make life easier to dilute these 1:1 with hot water to make them more pourable when making cocktails.

Jam/Marmalade

Whether home-made (see page 94) or store bought, a spoonful of jam or marmalade can add a fruity punch of sweetness to drinks. Lime marmalade is my secret weapon for a next-level Gimlet.

ACIDS

The ying to sweet's yang, every cocktail needs either some bitterness or some acid to balance it. Acid adds a tartness that whets the appetite and keeps you coming back for more. Traditionally, citrus has been used in this capacity in cocktails, but what do you do if you don't have a lemon or lime around?

Vinegar

While 'vinegary' might not sound like a complementary flavour note in most situations, it can be a very useful tool in adding acid. I'm not suggesting you pop in 30 ml (1 oz) of vinegar instead of lemon juice, but it can be used in home-made ingredients – specifically shrubs – for extra pop. Apple-cider vinegar works in most situations, but it can be fun to play around with it. Champagne or white-wine vinegar is more delicate, or a fruit vinegar can add a different tone; for instance, I love using pineapple vinegar in a pineapple shrub. Even a little pickle brine can work wonders!

Powdered acids

We live in a modern world, so let's look to modern solutions. Most naturally occurring acids can be bought in powder form now, and while they're definitely not essential for at-home cocktail-making they can be quite useful. Citric acid is found in the usual acidic components of cocktails – lemon and lime – so provides the same zing. Malic acid has a softer acidity and is derived from fruits like apples and grapes. Tartaric acid is also found in grapes and gives a particularly wine-y tang. Ascorbic acid helps retain freshness in home-made ingredients; it stops them turning brown. Lactic acid is a by-product of fermentation and adds a savoury edge. These can be ordered from specialist stores and used as solutions straight in the cocktail, or as ingredients in prep recipes.

Verjus (or verjuice)

This is one of my favourite cocktail ingredients. It's essentially unripe grape juice, or unfermented wine, and has similar acidity to citrus but in a subtler, more nuanced way. Because its acidic bite comes from tartaric acid, it is a little softer and drier, and it can change depending on the varietal of the grapes used. It behaves the same as wine as well; it's shelf stable until opened, at which point it should be kept in the fridge for up to one month.

SALT

Salt is as important to cocktails as it is to cooking – technically, this belongs in the 'spice rack' section below, but it's so important I decided it deserved its own section.

I may espouse the Taste Triangle of strong, sweet, and bitter or sour, but salt and umami can really level up a cocktail, too. In small quantities, salt doesn't make things 'salty', but rather interferes with our experience of the other tastes. It increases our perception of sweetness by diminishing our ability to taste bitterness, hence why salting something like a grapefruit can actually make it more palatable. It also interacts with water in a way that makes it easier for volatile molecules to 'launch' themselves in the air, which is a rather dramatic-sounding way of saying it will heighten aromas. These qualities combined can mean, essentially, that salt makes things taste like the best version of themselves and leaves us literally salivating – always a good outcome in the world of cocktail creation.

Salt

A natural, larger-grained salt like sea salt or kosher salt is easier to control than table salt, which is more concentrated. It can be used for salt rims, as on a Margarita, or to season home-made ingredients. You can also turn it into a saline solution to make it easier to incorporate into cocktails. Salt also plays a major role in preserves and ferments (see page 94) which can add complexity to your libations.

Salty sauces

Salty sauces, such as Worcestershire, soy, Maggi seasoning, etc. are good for more than just Bloody Marys and Micheladas. Used judiciously, they can add an umami kick to all sorts of drinks, so think outside the box!

SPICE RACK

Spices are a pretty major weapon in your arsenal when it comes to upgrading home-made delights. Sure, raspberries and sugar can make a great syrup, but add some cinnamon and cloves and it's suddenly a perfect fit for whisky or rum; add chilli flakes and star anise and tequila has met its match.

Get as creative as you like, and try using the flavour pairings section on page 45 to spark some inspiration. I generally prefer working with whole spices rather than powders for things like cinnamon, nutmeg, vanilla, star anise and peppercorns as they're just a bit easier to control, but powders are fine if that's all you have. The more you have, the more adventurous you can be, but here are some non-negotiables for me:

Cinnamon sticks

Cinnamon mimics a lot of the flavours that come from barrel-ageing, so it pairs perfectly with basically any aged spirit.

Whole nutmeg

Using a microplane to grate fresh nutmeg as opposed to using powder gives a stronger, fresher flavour.

Star anise

This is a good way to add a warm, herbal undertone if you don't have any fresh herbs.

Peppercorns

Black pepper is great, of course, but I also love using pink peppercorns if you can find them (they're a bit softer and sweeter). Things like Sichuan or sancho pepper can give a delicious kick as well, and give your cocktail a sense of the exotic.

Cardamom

Cardamom is delicious in small quantities but can overtake quite quickly, so just be careful how much you use and how long you infuse it for. I generally lightly bash the pods but keep them whole so they are easier to pull out if the flavour becomes overwhelming.

Chilli/Hot sauce

Chilli flakes are good to have on hand, as are dried whole chillies, like chipotle or anchos. It also helps to have a couple of hot sauces at your disposal – even just a bottle of Tabasco can make a pretty banging spicy Marg', but you can also find ones that are tailored to the cocktails you are making, like a mango and habanero hot sauce.

Vanilla

Beans are great and last quite a while, but they can be expensive. If you can find a good-quality extract or paste made from real vanilla beans, that can work well too, but steer clear of essence as it tends to be artificial.

Ginger

Again, fresh ginger is ideal but a jar of chopped or even pickled ginger is a great back-up option for adding that zing.

Tamarind

Tamarind puree has a moreish sweet-and-sour flavour that adds both sweetness and acidity – I use it a lot in cooking (try it in your next curry or stir-fry and thank me later!) – but it also works really well with rums and whiskies and can give your cocktail a little Asian-style flair.

TEA TIME

Teas are a great and easy way to add flavour and structure to a drink. You can use loose-leaf teas in syrups and infusions (see page 76), or just brew it and use it as a dilution element. Some teas contain tannin, which adds a drying sensation in cocktails and can be used to great effect in non-alcoholic drinks to add the body that would otherwise be provided by the alcohol.

Black teas

These contain the most tannin, so you do have to be careful when brewing them that they don't become too astringent. I like to have regular breakfast tea and Earl Grey around. Chai can be great to layer in spice as well.

Green teas

Green teas tend to have low tannins, but still have a distinctive 'tea' flavour while being lighter and brighter than black teas. Sencha and jasmine both have great flavour profiles for cocktails.

Herbal teas

These are an easy way to add flavourings to cocktails – they don't tend to have caffeine or tannin so are basically a nice way to season the dilution in your cocktail. I'm a fan of lemongrass and ginger, or hibiscus, as they both work well with a variety of spirits, but there are plenty to experiment with!

FROZEN FAVOURITES

Ah the freezer, the eternal saviour of the perennially lazy ... I mean, waste conscious! While I love using fresh ingredients, it's just not always possible to have a fully stocked fruit bowl – but there can always be a reasonably stocked freezer drawer.

Fruits

Frozen fruits, like mango, bananas and berries, taste *almost* as good as fresh, and if you're going to use them in a syrup or shrub, for instance, the difference is pretty negligible. Using frozen also helps to limit waste as you can just use what you need at the time.

Ice cubes

We'll go into more detail on page 42, but using ice-cube trays to store left-over teas, juices, herbs or even cocktails can give you little flavour bombs to play with in future drinks.

Ice cream

Ice cream can be used to add dairy to drinks; you don't need to have fresh milk or cream around to make Grasshoppers, White Russians or a Brandy Alexander. Just chuck a scoop of ice cream in!

CANS AND JARS

I completely understand the mantra of 'fresh is best'. For years, the bar world worked hard to counter the idea that cocktails were artificial, sweet-and-sour mix concoctions, but we don't have to fall on our organically grown heirloom sword. Especially in the comfort of your own home, shortcuts are allowed and, quite honestly, using preserved ingredients can sometimes taste better.

Tinned fruit

I *always* have a couple of tins of passionfruit pulp in my cupboard; I love it for a tropical pop. When I feel like I need a holiday (but I can't afford one), I add it to basically anything: a Daiquiri, Margarita, Mai Tai – crank the heating and chill out. Tinned peaches, pears and lychees, etc. can all be used to great effect either straight in the cocktail shaker or as the base for home-made ingredients.

Pickles

Of course, you can make your own (and I do encourage you to – see page 124), but having a jar of good-quality olives and pickled onions within reach will mean that your Martini needs can always be met. The brine can also be used to add all-important salt to cocktails (see page 125). In a pinch I've even deployed capers and cornichons; creativity comes in many forms.

Coconut milk/cream

Coconut milk or cream is the key player in a Piña Colada, but preserved versions can also be used to add texture to many a cocktail, particularly blended ones. It also works well as a vegan alternative to dairy in cocktail recipes.

Long-life juices

Okay, I'm just going to say it: I prefer long-life pineapple juice to fresh. It's less messy and more consistent. No one can guarantee a perfectly ripe pineapple every time you want a Piña Colada, but a bottle of pineapple juice in your cupboard will always do the trick. We don't always plan our hangovers, so shelf-stable tomato juice is also great to have ... you know, just in case. Some juices like grapefruit are undeniably better fresh, but having a stabilised back-up option is just smart.

PREP SHIFT

There are a few references in this book to 'prep', and this is just bar speak for preparation. Your 'prep recipes' are home-made ingredients you make ahead of time to have ready for when cocktail hour hits. A 'prep shift' in a bar is essentially like meal prepping: done ahead of service, you get all of your syrups, shrubs and infusions ready to prepare you for busy services throughout the week. While you don't have to be quite as diligent as this at home, spending a few hours pottering around your kitchen making a shrub or a sherbet to stock your fridge or freezer with can provide you with ready-made flavour-makers poised to be deployed at a moment's notice the next time you want to wow your guests (or treat yourself!).

So, what equipment do you need to be able to whip these up when the mood strikes?

Saucepans

It's probably pretty obvious, but a couple of decent-sized saucepans with lids are invaluable for all sorts of recipes.

Strainer

A regular fine-mesh sieve will suffice for most recipes, and the finer the better, as a colander or a wider mesh can allow particles through that you don't want. To make life easier, try to find one that will fit securely over whatever jugs or bowls you will be pouring into (this is coming from someone who has not yet mastered a one-handed pour!). It can be helpful to have some muslin (cheesecloth) and/or large coffee filters around to filter anything you don't want to be cloudy.

Knife/Peeler/Microplane

For actual bartending (cutting wedges, garnishes and so on) I usually use a small, serrated knife, but it's helpful to have a big, sharp knife for prep, especially if you will be grappling with larger fruits like pineapples. A good peeler for skins is also a solid investment, and a microplane grater is practical for adding citrus zests or spices like nutmeg to your recipes.

Juicer(s)

For just lemon and lime juice, you can probably get by with some elbow grease and a citrus press, but you can get some quite cheap electric citrus juicers if you do entertain a lot. Other fresh juices (melon, pineapple, cucumber, carrot, etc.) can be delicious to use in cocktails but you will have to invest in a centrifugal juicer. In the recipes in this book, I've tried to steer clear of using too many juices that can't easily be found at the shops.

Measuring jugs

I like to have a few different sizes: a smaller one (500 ml/17 oz or less) for precision and a larger one (2 litre/68 oz or, if you have the space, 5 litre/169 oz) for straining into and batching. A medium-sized one (1 litre/34 oz) is also handy as it fits a whole bottle of booze in it, so can be used for infusions. Try to find ones with good pouring spouts to avoid mess. I also often use jiggers for smaller amounts of liquid.

Scale

A decent kitchen scale, able to measure smaller amounts accurately, is useful for portioning dry ingredients.

Bowls

I love bowls. Whether cooking or doing cocktail prep, having plenty of bowls means you can have everything chopped and measured out before you actually start, so you're less likely to forget something. A set of metal or glass nesting bowls is a must!

Blender

Rather than muddling everything, it can be useful to have a blender to make recipes like fruit purees so they are pourable and can be easily added to cocktails. Of course, you can make frozen drinks in it, too.

Funnel

This is one of those things you can definitely live without but having one makes pouring and decanting infinitely easier, especially if you're uncoordinated like me! Use it to decant liquids into storage bottles.

Containers/Bottles

Once you've made your delicious concoctions, you'll need to store them. The most cost-effective way is just to save glass bottles, clean and refill them – make sure to hang onto the lids, too. Otherwise, you can invest in some swing-top bottles. Think about what storage space you have available to you; it might make more sense, for instance, to store things in stackable tubs in the fridge and decant into a bottle (using your funnel, *wink wink*) when you're actually going to use them. Squeezy bottles with nozzles are useful for thicker ingredients like purees (if the nozzle tip is too fine and you're struggling to get anything out, just cut it off a little further down where it's wider), and dropper bottles are best for tinctures and bitters. Small clip-top jars are good for ferments, pickles and so on. You might also want to invest in some bigger jars with a spout if you plan to mix cocktails in larger batches ahead of time (more on that on page 43).

Ice-cube trays/Moulds

Almost all drinks need ice, and you often need more than you think so remember to keep on top of your ice program. If you can, turn the ice cubes out and refill the trays as often as you remember in order to build up a store of ice, but as a minimum, remember to refill them after every use. It can be useful to have a few different sizes: some smaller trays (like the ones that come with your freezer) for blending and highballs, bigger cubes (around 3.5 cm/1½ in) for shaking and stirring, and large blocks or spheres (around 5 cm/2 in, or whatever fits well in your glasses) for serving 'on the rocks'.

Hot tip (literally): try boiling your water before freezing to remove impurities and make your ice clearer.

Now look, I'm not your mum, but my number one tip is to clean as you go; there's nothing more stressful than a messy kitchen or workspace when you actually get to the point of making drinks. Which leads us to …

SERVICE

Once all your prep is done, it's time to get ready for 'service', i.e. actually making the drinks. Let's take a look at the equipment you'll need for mixing up a storm, plus some handy hints for serving lots of cocktails at once while still making sure they look great.

BAR EQUIPMENT MUST-HAVES

Jigger

This is my number one must-have. While you might feel generous free-pouring your cocktails instead of using a jigger, you and your guests won't thank you for the headache the next day. Plus, it's just really hard to make balanced drinks without one. My favourite is a graduated jigger: a larger 75 ml (2½ oz) jigger which is marked in 15 ml (½ oz) increments. This makes it easier to make multiple cocktails at once, or if you want to batch them ahead of time, you can measure the whole cocktail out at once.

Shaker tins/Mixing glass

Shaking cocktails aerates and dilutes them, so it's important for a lot of recipes. I recommend 'tin on tin' Boston shakers, and to have a few of them (you can find ones that are relatively inexpensive). Even if you can only shake one tin at a time, it's much quicker to pour all the ingredients at once into separate tins and then shake them one by one rather than building then shaking, building then shaking ... 'Tin on tin' Bostons are big enough to make two (or even three at a squeeze) drinks at once, they're painless to clean and they stack for easy storage. Saying that, at a pinch, I've had some great drinks shaken up in a protein shaker bottle or an airtight container, too!

If you make a lot of 'stirred' drinks it might be worth investing in a mixing glass, but they're not as necessary; you can just stir drinks in one half of your shaker tins. In fact, a lot of high-end bars do this now anyway, as metal chills drinks faster and slows dilution. So, you're not being cheap if you forego the glass – you're just being scientific!

Strainers

Being perfectly honest, for my own brand of lazy, at-home bartending, I'm a big fan of the 'shake and dump': just pouring everything out of the shaker into the glass for a crushed-ice effect. But, of course, that doesn't work for everything, so have a Hawthorne strainer (the spring allows it to fit into different-sized tins and glasses) on hand for when you want to serve a drink 'up' (i.e. not on ice). A fine strainer is useful for straining out smaller chips of ice (and for removing any pulp, etc.) from home-made ingredients for a smoother texture.

Bar spoon

A bar spoon is great for mixing cocktails, of course, but you can also use it to measure smaller quantities; the spoon itself is usually 5 ml (⅛ oz). The long handle means I often use it to stir hot things, too, for example when stirring hot water and sugar to make sugar syrup.

Knife/Peeler and chopping board

A small, serrated knife and vegetable peeler will cover most of your garnish creation needs. A microplane can also be used for grating nutmeg, chocolate and so on.

There are, of course, lots of other bits and pieces that can be useful – muddlers, tongs, tweezers, skewers, etc. – but none are essential. Start with the basics listed above and collect these other tools along the way if you decide they're something that you would like to have.

GLASSWARE MUST-HAVES

Glassware is where you can really have some fun! I never pass an op shop or vintage market without checking out their glassware, and have scored some really beautiful pieces. With that in mind, don't stress too much about the shape of your glasses; a Martini tastes perfectly good out of a champagne flute instead of a martini glass, I can assure you from experience. However, glassware is a situation where size does matter. Too big and your serves will look stingy, too small and you'll have cocktails overflowing all over your carpet.

Rocks glass/Lowball

Short, stemless and fairly wide, rocks glasses can hold a spirit mixer, cocktail on the rocks or neat spirit. If you will only be serving drinks with ice in them, look for a larger size, sometimes known as a 'double rocks' or 'double Old Fashioned' glass – around 350 ml (12 oz) is a good size for most serves. Personally, I like something with a bit of weight to it as it tends to be stirred down. Usually, rocks glasses are reserved for more serious drinks, so the glass needs to have similar gravitas.

Tall glass/Highball

Tall and narrow, these glasses are particularly good for bubbly drinks (they're sometimes known as Collins glasses after the Tom Collins, which is topped up with soda water/club soda). I also tend to go for something around 300–400 ml (10–13½ oz) here, and not much larger. A lot of drinks served in highballs are built in the glass then topped up, so erring on the smaller side ensures you won't overwhelm your cocktail with mixer.

Stemmed cocktail glass

Whether you love the angular modernity of a V-shaped Martini glass, the classic curves of a coupe or the vintage glamour of a Nick & Nora, a stemmed cocktail glass adds a sense of occasion to any drink. Used for drinks served 'up' (i.e. not on ice), the stem keeps your hands away from the liquid, helping to keep it colder for longer. As legendary bartender Harry Craddock is reputed to have said, 'the best way to drink a cocktail is quickly, while it's still laughing at you' (and also still cold), so steer clear of the novelty oversized ones and stick to something around 150–200 ml (5–7 oz), and just make yourself a second drink instead!

Of course, if you love drinking Moscow Mules it might be worth investing in some copper mugs, for example, but a selection of the above glassware will allow you to serve any cocktail in a fitting manner.

GARNISH TRAY

You drink with your eyes first, so presenting your cocktails in an aesthetically pleasing way is important. Some garnishes, like citrus twists or herbs, act as an ingredient in the cocktail; the aroma they bring elevates the experience and can bring the whole drink together. Others, like a twirly straw, are just decorative embellishments – and that's okay! Cocktails should be fun, so add that paper umbrella if it will brighten your day!

Fresh citrus

Citrus adds a joyful pop of colour and flavour as a garnish. Twists are more for the scent contained in the oils that are spritzed over the surface of the drink, whereas putting pieces of fruit in the drink will infuse the flavour of the citrus in the drink itself. Wedges can be squeezed in, and work to adjust the zinginess of the drink to personal preference, or wheels can be suspended through the drink to picturesque effect. Lemons and limes are classic, but oranges can bring a softer, sweeter note. My particular favourite, grapefruit, adds a perfumed bitterness. When in season, fruits like blood orange or mandarin can provide a fun spin, too.

Other fruits and veggies

Garnishes can also provide a visual cue as to what is in the drink; nothing says tropical flavours like a wedge of pineapple on the side of your glass! Cucumbers and rhubarb can be peeled lengthways with a veggie peeler and rolled to make a dainty scroll. Slices of chilli or pepper can indicate something is a little spicier, and nothing suggests refreshment more than an apple fan.

Herb garden

Fresh herbs are fragrant and beautiful. They also require minimal effort – no slicing or dicing necessary – so are a great option when serving lots of drinks. Herbs can be pricey, so if you want to make sure you have fresh herbs on hand when it's cocktail o'clock, consider growing a small herb garden or planting some in pots so they're easy to pick as you need them. Mint is a time-honoured addition to many drinks, but I also like using savoury herbs, like thyme or rosemary, as a counterpoint in fruity drinks. Dill, basil and sage are other top picks (pun intended) to add interest. Use the Flavour friends section on page 45 to choose the perfect match for your drink.

Dehydrated fruit

While it doesn't bring the flavour and aroma of fresh fruit, dehydrated fruit is pretty to look at and, importantly, shelf stable, making it ideal to have in the cupboard for when it's out of season or you're caught without fresh. You can buy dehydrated citrus garnishes, but dehydrating fruit yourself is a good way to save some money and use up any left-over fruit you might have. A dehydrator obviously makes it easier, but it can also be done in the oven at a low temperature over several hours. For citrus wheels, cut the citrus into 5 mm–1 cm (¼–½ in) slices (or as fine as you can manage – using a mandolin makes this easier). Lay them on a baking tray lined with baking paper and spritz the fruit with lemon juice to help it retain its colour. Place in the oven on its lowest heat and bake for 3–5 hours until they are fully dehydrated. Turn them occasionally to ensure they dry evenly and don't stick. Lemon, lime and orange wheels make great dehydrated garnishes, but so do apples, pineapples, strawberries, and even cucumber – if it can be sliced, it can be dried.

Decorative ice cubes

Another clever way to save on waste is to freeze your garnishes. Fill an ice-cube mould with berries, herbs, edible flowers or slices of chilli or cucumber, top up with water and stick in the freezer. They'll be ready to beautify your drink whenever you need them!

Rims

We all love a salt rim on a Margarita, but why stop there? I always have some Tajin on hand to add a spicy-limey tang, or cinnamon sugar for a dessert-style cocktail, but you can also make bespoke rims. Simply add your own seasoning (finely chopped or blitzed spices, herbs or zest) to sugar or salt to amplify the flavours in the drink.

Cherries/Olives/Pickles

A good-quality jar of each is essential for every home bar.

Most of all, get creative! I usually have an eye on sustainability as well and try not to use something only for garnish. If you're making Old Fashioneds with an orange twist one night, then fresh orange juice Mimosas should be on the menu the next morning! I also salvage ingredients where I can from prep recipes. For instance, if I am making the Blueberry and lemongrass shrub on page 89, I keep the blueberries once the shrub is strained off and skewer them for use in the drink itself. Fresh garnishes can be prepared a little ahead of time if you're going to be making multiple drinks. Simply cover with a damp cloth and they'll last a couple of hours. It will help take the stress out of slicing, peeling and skewering à la minute.

Which brings us to ...

HOST WITH THE MOST

Even the most consummate host can get a little flustered when entertaining, so getting a head start can take the pressure off and let you relax with your friends. All of the prep recipes in this book can be made well ahead of time. If you regularly make cocktails at home, I would even suggest setting a day aside once every month or so and tackling some prep recipes which can then be stored in the fridge, freezer or pantry until you need them. Here are some other recommendations for hosting groups with ease.

Workspace set-up

I totally understand that at-home cocktail making is often a spontaneous endeavour, and believe me I've had many off-the-cuff drinks made in a messy kitchen at midnight which have totally hit the mark. But, generally speaking, having a space set aside where you can pull out the bottles and other ingredients and equipment that you'll need is helpful. If it can be near a bin, sink and the freezer with ice that's ideal, otherwise consider setting up a dump bucket and ice bucket to save you trekking back and forth to the kitchen. Try to pre-squeeze any juice you need and organise your garnishes. Do a little stocktake of your glassware. It doesn't have to be matching, but you do need at least one glass per guest ... unless you're *very* good friends.

Write a menu

Nobody expects to go to a friend's house and order their meal à la carte, but they might expect to be able to request any drink they fancy if you have a well-stocked bar. Next thing you know, six guests arrive at once and ask for six different drinks, and you're stressed. Having a little menu written up can help guide them towards drinks you've prepared for, and it makes a nice keepsake for your events. Consider the number of guests you're expecting; I tend to steer clear of any shaken drinks for groups of six or more to save my arms. If you must offer a Margarita or Daiquiri-type drink, bust out the blender.

Group serves/Batching

You can use the aforementioned menu to make life easier for yourself. Having a designated welcome cocktail that you know you can sling out easily will ensure everybody has a drink in their hands within a few moments of arriving. Punches (see page 182) can work well for this, or a low-ABV Spritz or Collins-style serve (see page 144), which can be built in glasses ready for ice, then garnished as your guests trickle in.

You can also batch the other drinks you'd like to offer by multiplying the ingredients in the recipe by the number you expect to serve. If you leave fresh ingredients out (i.e. only batch the alcohol and more stable ingredients) you can do it well ahead of time, or store for your next party if you don't use it all. Simply add any fresh citrus juice, fizzy ingredients (soda water/club soda, sparkling wine or other mixers) or garnishes as you're making the drink. That way you can mix drinks by only pouring from the batch bottle instead of having to measure out three or four different ingredients.

Above all, remember to have fun! Assuming your guests aren't paying – or just like to wind you up – they're not going to mind if you run out of an ingredient and have to switch to something else, if your twists are a little wonky, or if they have to wait a few minutes while you craft them a new creative concoction. They'll remember good times with friends and delicious drinks – you provide the former, and this book will help with the latter.

FLAVOUR FRIENDS

You can't name a more iconic duo than gin and tonic, and the reason they work so well together is actually scientific; the molecular compounds in gin (specifically the alpha-pinene and limonene found in juniper) and quinine in tonic have an intense case of mutual attraction. This means that when their molecules get to bump and grind, they create new flavour molecules, which is why a G&T is such a different flavour sensation than drinking either gin or tonic water alone. Who says science isn't sexy?

This same principle can be applied to flavour pairings in general. Given that around 80–90 per cent of what we perceive as taste is actually smell, aroma compounds are particularly important here. A scientist from Firmenich (the world's largest privately owned fragrance and taste company), Franí§ois Benzi, was the first to suggest that if the major volatile compounds – i.e. the ones that jump up your nostrils – in two foods were similar, they might taste good together. The example he used was jasmine and pork liver, which both contain indole, and it turns out … they work! This technique is used a lot by chefs, notably Heston Blumenthal, who built his brand on surprising and delighting with unusual flavour combinations, like caviar and white chocolate – and now you can, too.

Of course, the best flavour friendships are not too different from human ones, with some areas of commonality, but a little bit of contrast as well. Sure, raspberries go well with other berries like strawberries and cherries, but your drink could be somewhat one dimensional if you just keep adding these similar flavours. Adding lemongrass, on the other hand, will bring a citrus and herbal note alongside the shared sweetness and florals, which will, in turn, bring out the best in the raspberry. So I like to look at both complementary and contrasting flavour pairings which can be layered to delicious effect.

There are lots of online resources and books on this subject depending on how deep you want to delve, but here we're going to concentrate on applying this idea to drinks by looking at how commonly used cocktail ingredients pair well with other flavours. As Niki Segnit says in *The Flavour Thesaurus*, 'one of the great satisfactions of discovering more about flavour combinations is the confidence it gives you to strike out on your own. Following the instructions in a recipe is like parroting pre-formed sentences from a phrasebook. Forming an understanding of how flavours work together, on the other hand, is like learning the language; it allows you to express yourself freely, to improvise, to find appropriate substitutions for ingredients, to cook a dish (or in this case, a cocktail) the way you fancy cooking it.' Hear, hear! And cin cin!

Using these infographics for inspiration, you can scour your local market for seasonal produce or have a rummage in your pantry or herb garden and bring an aspect of the unexpected to your drinks creations. Often just one extra element will elevate your drink from 'standard' to 'wow'!

How to use these charts

First of all, always keep the Taste Triangle in mind; every cocktail needs an element of strong, sweet, and bitter or sour to be balanced. Think of the items in these charts as building blocks of flavour that build the sides of the triangle.

Because I always encourage you to substitute on the fly, I find it useful to group ingredients by what they bring to a cocktail, such as sweetness or acid. This way, if something you want to use isn't on hand or is running low, you can see at a glance some other options that could bring a similar vibe to the drink.

The rest of the charts (see pages 56–60) show how commonly used spirits match with these broader categories and other modifiers, and you can use them to spark inspiration for your own cocktail creations.

TASTING SPIRITS TO SELECT COMPLEMENTARY FLAVOURS

I've had to work in broad brushstrokes in this book – as it's impossible to cover it all – with the most common flavour profiles for each spirit category, but I highly encourage you to taste and lean into the individual flavour of each ingredient you have. You might find a particular blended whisky, for example, that has a prominent chocolate note on top of the usual caramel and fruit flavours, which you might choose to enhance with berries, as chocolate and berries are a match made in heaven.

To taste spirits, pour a small amount into a tasting glass (ideally something with a curved shape that will funnel the aromas up towards your nose), and let it breathe for a minute. Alcohol is very volatile, so it can be all you smell when you first pour a spirit. Smell gently, with your mouth open, to allow the alcohol to cycle out. Take a small sip and allow it to roll around your mouth, hitting all of your tastebuds. Pay attention to the flavours you detect at the beginning, middle and end of the sip, as they often change. It can be useful to jot down your thoughts as you are doing this, and don't be afraid to add a little water if you find it too harsh; cocktails are diluted anyway!

Before mixing entire cocktails, I will often first sample each ingredient I intend to use side by side; if they smell and taste good one after the other, they will probably be friends in the glass. This can save the effort and wastage of mixing a whole drink just to realise the flavours are actually quite jarring together.

FLAVOUR

/ˈfleɪvə/

noun

the distinctive taste of a food or drink
an indication of the essential character
of something

verb

alter or enhance the taste of (food or drink)
by adding a particular ingredient

INGREDIENTS CHARTS

NOTE

This is not a scientific guide. The categories were determined purely by flavour profile as opposed to the botanical family they technically belong to or any other factor. Some ingredients would arguably fit into a couple of different categories, but this book had to be published at some point, so decisions had to be made.

Seasonality is important to consider here, but of course you can use the prep recipes (see page 63) to preserve produce at its peak to enjoy all year round. Some of the fruit, vegetables, herbs and spices I've included are a little left-of-centre, but all are ones I've seen used to great effect in drinks, so if you can get your hands on them, I encourage you to get creative and think outside the box!

FRUIT

Citrus fruit

+ Lemon, lime, orange, grapefruit, mandarin, cumquat, yuzu

Berries

+ Strawberry, raspberry, blueberry, blackberry, cherry, red grape, açai, goji, fig, lychee

Stone fruit

+ Peach, plum/prune, nectarine, apricot

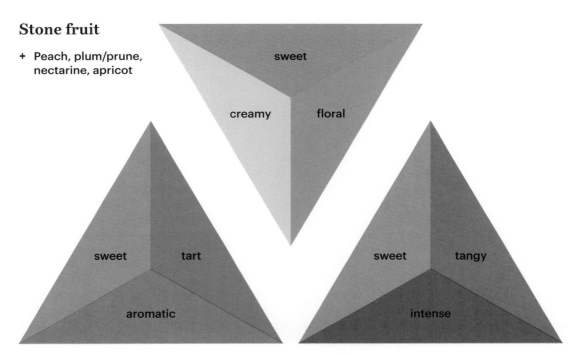

Orchard fruit

+ Apple, pear, quince, nashi pear, kiwi, rhubarb, green grape

Tropical fruit

+ Pineapple, passionfruit, coconut, banana, guava, pomegranate, mango, melon

VEGETABLES

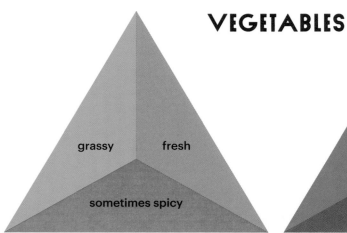

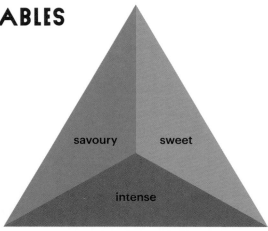

Aromatic vegetables

+ Celery, fennel, capsicum (bell pepper), chilli, ginger, pea, cucumber

Earthy vegetables

+ Tomato, carrot, beetroot (beet), mushroom, artichoke, olive

SPICES

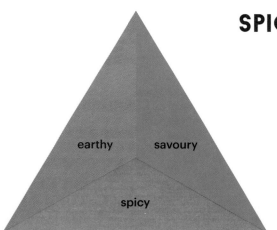

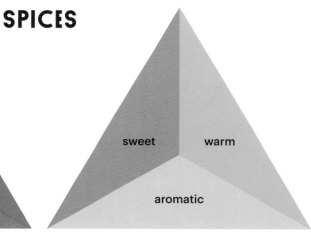

Spicy spices

+ Peppercorn, smoked paprika, fennel seed, turmeric, cayenne pepper, juniper, cumin

Baking spices

+ Cinnamon, clove, cardamom, nutmeg, allspice, star anise, vanilla, cacao, tamarind

HERBS

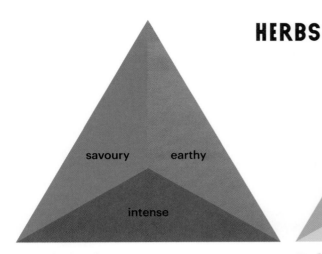

savoury **earthy**

intense

Hardy herbs

+ Rosemary, thyme, bay, lavender, tarragon, pine, sea herbs

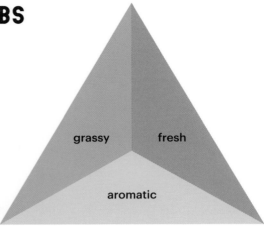

grassy **fresh**

aromatic

Delicate herbs

+ Mint, basil, dill, sage, coriander (cilantro), lemongrass, shiso, eucalyptus

OTHER

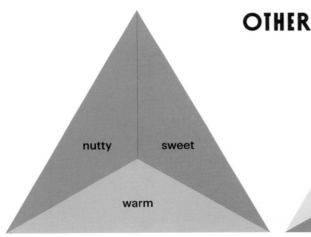

nutty **sweet**

warm

Nuts

+ Almond, hazelnut, pistachio nut, walnut, pecan, macadamia

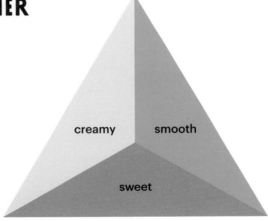

creamy **smooth**

sweet

Dairy and replacements

+ Butter, milk, cream, ice cream, coconut milk/cream, kefir, yoghurt, buttermilk, almond milk

NOTE

I have not included dairy in the cocktail charts that follow, because it takes a drink down a whole other, distinct path.

COCKTAIL CHARTS

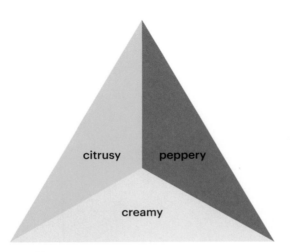

Vodka

+ **Plays well with: fino or manzanilla sherry, dry vermouth, citrus or floral amaro**

Option 1: Berry + Citrus fruit + Delicate herb
Option 2: Earthy vegetable + Spicy spice
Option 3: Orchard fruit + Aromatic vegetable

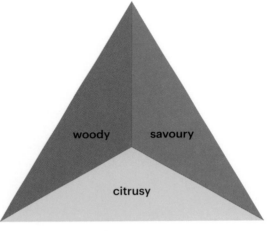

London Dry gin

+ **Plays well with: fino, manzanilla or amontillado sherry, all vermouth, sake, citrus or vegetal amaro**

Option 1: Citrus fruit + Hardy herb
Option 2: Stone fruit + Delicate herb
Option 3: Tropical fruit + Baking spice + Hardy herb

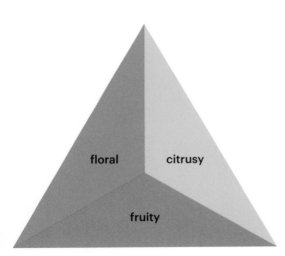

Contemporary gin

+ **Plays well with: fino or manzanilla sherry, dry or off-dry vermouth, sake, citrus or floral amaro**

Option 1: Orchard fruit + Delicate herb
Option 2: Citrus fruit + Delicate herb
Option 3: Berry + Aromatic vegetable

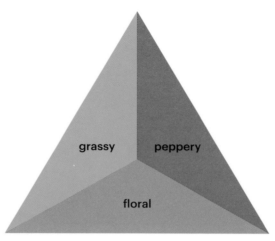

Blanco tequila

+ Plays well with: fino or manzanilla sherry, dry or off-dry vermouth, citrus amaro, mezcal

Option 1: Earthy vegetable + Spicy spice + Delicate herb
Option 2: Citrus fruit + Aromatic vegetable
Option 3: Tropical fruit + Baking spice + Hardy herb

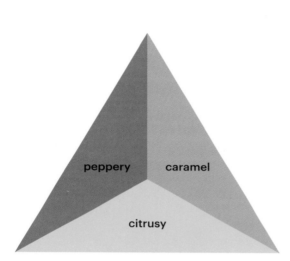

Aged tequila

+ Plays well with: amontillado or oloroso sherry, off-dry or sweet vermouth, citrus or vegetal amaro, mezcal

Option 1: Stone fruit + Spicy spice + Delicate herb
Option 2: Citrus fruit + Baking spice
Option 3: Tropical fruit + Hardy herb

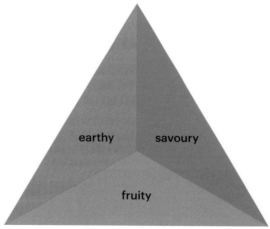

Mezcal

+ Plays well with: amontillado or oloroso sherry, off-dry or sweet vermouth, port and madeira, citrus or vegetal amaro, tequila

Option 1: Stone fruit + Spicy spice + Hardy herb
Option 2: Tropical fruit + Hardy herb
Option 3: Citrus fruit + Delicate herb + Nut

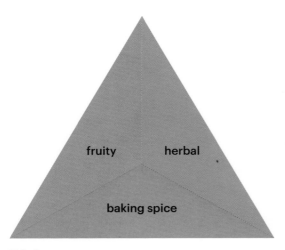

Lighter rum

+ **Plays well with: fino or amontillado sherry, dry or off-dry vermouth, white port, citrus amaro, other rum**

Option 1: Tropical fruit + Delicate herb
Option 2: Aromatic vegetable + Stone fruit + Nut
Option 3: Citrus fruit + Baking spice

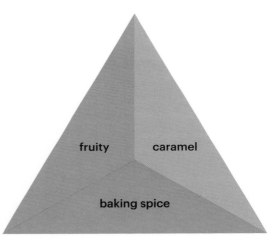

Heavier rum

+ **Plays well with: amontillado or oloroso sherry, off-dry or sweet vermouth, port and madeira, citrus or vegetal amaro, other rum**

Option 1: Tropical fruit + Hardy herb
Option 2: Stone fruit + Baking spice
Option 3: Citrus fruit + Nut + Delicate herb

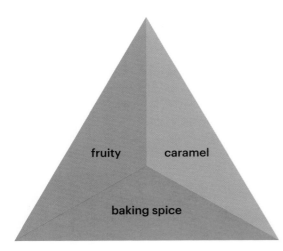

Brandy

+ **Plays well with: amontillado, oloroso or sweet sherry, off-dry or sweet vermouth, port and madeira, citrus or floral amaro**

Option 1: Citrus fruit + Berry + Baking spice
Option 2: Orchard fruit + Nut
Option 3: Stone fruit + Delicate herb

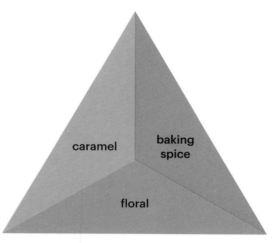

Bourbon

+ Plays well with: amontillado, oloroso or sweet sherry, off-dry or sweet vermouth, port and madeira, citrus or vegetal amaro

Option 1: Berry + Delicate herb + Nut
Option 2: Stone fruit + Spicy spice
Option 3: Orchard fruit + Baking spice

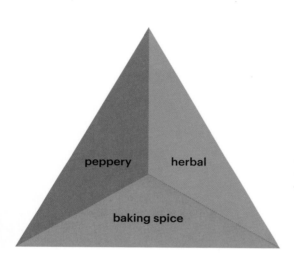

Rye

+ Plays well with: amontillado, oloroso or sweet sherry, all vermouth, port and madeira, citrus or vegetal amaro, heavier rum, other whiskies

Option 1: Berry + Baking spice + Hardy herb
Option 2: Orchard fruit + Delicate herb + Nut
Option 3: Stone fruit + Aromatic vegetable

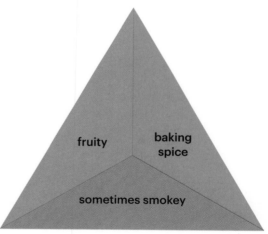

Blended whisky

+ Plays well with: amontillado, oloroso or sweet sherry, off-dry or sweet vermouth, port and madeira, citrus or floral amaro

Option 1: Berry + Nut + Delicate herb
Option 2: Stone fruit + Delicate herb
Option 3: Orchard fruit + Baking spice

PREP
RECIPES

There are some time-honoured techniques to add extra flavour to your drinks – here we will explore them with minimal mess and fuss. The idea is that each of the recipes in this section teaches you a method of flavour-making and you can apply this method to the flavour combinations of your choice. Preparing these simple recipes ahead of time means you can create interesting cocktails easily and quickly. It's how bars and restaurants do it, so I'm letting you in on our secrets!

If you do have access to local, seasonal produce, make the most of it. Buying in-season fruit and vegetables means you can enjoy produce at its peak of flavour, and when it's most abundant and affordable. At my local market, suppliers often sell trays of ripe fruit for a song on the last day of the week. Ripe – or even overripe – fruit is packed full of flavour, which is ideal for fermenting or turning it into a shrub straight away. Frozen or tinned works too, so don't stress if that's all you have access to.

These recipes are all designed to be customisable. They're really more about the techniques, which can then be used to prepare whatever produce you have on hand. Use the Flavour friends charts (see page 45) for help with making scrumptious substitutions. I've also suggested other ingredients that work particularly well in some recipes.

Generally, these recipes will each make around 500 ml (17 oz) of the end product. This is enough for ten to twenty drinks depending on how much is used in the cocktail recipe. You can, of course, scale up or down from there. To be really precise, you can weigh liquid as well to make sure it's a true ratio. For example, for a 1:1 simple syrup you could weigh equal amounts of sugar and water instead of weighing the sugar and using a measuring jug for the water, but the difference is negligible.

Make sure your bottles or containers are sterilised, and always label them so you know what they contain and when you made it. If you want to freeze them, ice-cube moulds are a good way of portioning your ingredients, especially if you only tend to make a drink or two at a time. I've given an indication of how long each ingredient should last, but of course it will depend on how fresh the original produce is and how you store it, so use your common sense – if something smells or tastes not quite right, go with your gut and bin it.

PREPARATION

/prɛpəˈreɪʃən/

noun

the action or process of making something
ready for use or service or of getting ready
for some occasion

a substance that is specially made up,
especially a food or medicine (cocktails
count as medicine, right?)

SYRUPS AND CORDIALS

These are fun ways to make up the sweet side of the Taste Triangle. As much as 'sweet' is often considered a dirty word, a certain amount of sugar is necessary not only to balance a cocktail but also to add texture to a drink.

Syrups and cordials can be used pretty interchangeably. The main difference is that syrups are based on a combination of sugar and water with other flavours infused, whereas cordials are based on fruit juice. We're not too concerned about semantics here though, and they essentially achieve the same effect in a drink.

Tips and tricks for best results

+ These recipes have more in common with actual cooking than making drinks, so I encourage you to taste, taste and taste again! Keeping an eye on the development of the flavour through the process means you can make adjustments where necessary before you reach a point of no return.

+ Control your temperature. The more heat applied, the more 'cooked' or 'stewed' the final product will taste. For ingredients where you want to retain freshness, such as delicate herbs, consider just steeping them in cool syrup as opposed to heating them. In general, I prefer low and slow infusing instead of boiling quickly as it gives me more control.

+ When using spices, try to use whole ones; they are easier to scoop out if the flavour starts to become overwhelming. This applies to citrus peels, too; the longer you cook them, the more bitter they become, so using whole slices of peel as opposed to grated zest is a good way to control it, or you can add grated zest closer to the end. Citric acid could be used instead, too, for adding just a splash of brightness.

+ Less is more. A good rule of thumb when experimenting is to start with a 1:1 ratio of sugar to water or 0.5:1 sugar to fruit/fruit juice and increase from there; it's easier to add sugar than take it away! Same goes for any other ingredients: it's better to err on the side of caution and add more if the flavour isn't coming through.

HIBISCUS GRENADINE

Grenadine is a pomegranate syrup used a lot in classic cocktail recipes. While you can find some good-quality grenadines on the market, a lot are artificially hued and too sweet. By making it yourself at home you can retain a lot more of the pomegranate's tartness. Adding hibiscus elevates the floral notes and makes this an awesome addition to all manner of cocktails and mocktails.

PREP

You can juice pomegranates by adding the seeds to a blender, blitzing and then straining well through a fine-mesh sieve. If that all sounds like too much bother, I've had good results using bottled pomegranate juice, too.

Try instead

Leave out the hibiscus for a classic grenadine, or use other floral flavours, such as rosewater. Alternatively, baking spices work well (see page 54).

Pairs well with

Vodka, London Dry or contemporary gin, lighter or heavier rum, whiskies.

EQUIPMENT

measuring jug
peeler
scale
saucepan
fine-mesh sieve

INGREDIENTS

500 ml (17 oz) pomegranate juice

60 ml (2 oz) pomegranate molasses

5 ml (⅙ oz) orange-blossom water

2 strips lemon peel

500 g (1 lb 2 oz) granulated white sugar

30 g (1 oz) hibiscus flowers (loose-leaf hibiscus tea works well)

METHOD

Add all the ingredients, except the hibiscus, to your saucepan and stir over a low heat until combined. Simmer for about 20 minutes, until you have a syrupy consistency. Keep an eye on it and make sure it stays a pourable consistency; it will thicken as it cools. Take off the heat, remove the lemon peels and add the hibiscus to the syrup to infuse as the mixture cools. Taste the grenadine after an hour or two and, once the hibiscus flavour is as pronounced as you would like, strain into a container.

STORE

In the fridge for 1–2 weeks, or in the freezer for up to 3 months.

BEETROOT AND APPLE CORDIAL

The sweetness of beetroot (beet) and apple are a perfect match, with the beetroot providing an earthy base note and the apple a tart top note.

PREP

The hassle-free method is to buy pre-cooked baby beetroots as they have a more delicate flavour and are easier to grapple with. Otherwise, scrub, peel and steam either baby beets or regular beetroots until tender, then chop roughly. You can, of course, freshly squeeze your apples, but this recipe also works perfectly well with store-bought, additive-free apple juice (not from concentrate).

Try instead

Switch out the apple juice for orange, or the beetroot for carrot (in this case it's easier to juice the carrot raw and just combine with apple juice in equal parts). Ginger is a great addition, and it can be added towards the end of cooking and left to infuse.

Pairs well with

Vodka, London Dry or contemporary gin, blanco tequila, mezcal.

EQUIPMENT

scale

measuring jug

peeler

juicer

saucepan

strainer

INGREDIENTS

300 g (10½ oz) chopped beetroot (beet)

300 ml (10 oz) apple juice

300 g (10½ oz) granulated white sugar

pinch salt

peel and juice of 1 small lemon (about 45 ml/1½ oz)

METHOD

Add everything except the lemon juice to your saucepan and stir over a low heat until combined. Simmer for about 10 minutes until reduced to a syrupy consistency. You don't want the apple to taste 'stewed' so don't cook it for too long. Take off the heat, remove the lemon peel and stir in the lemon juice before straining.

STORE

In the fridge for 1–2 weeks, or in the freezer for up to 3 months.

RASPBERRY SYRUP WITH BASIL AND MINT

Raspberries are super versatile; they are floral enough to work with lighter spirits, but robust enough to stand up to darker spirits as well (one of my favourite desserts is the Scottish cranachan: oats and raspberries with whisky-spiked cream – you can thank me later, but I digress). Because of this, a good raspberry syrup can be layered with all manner of flavourings to tailor it to purpose. Here, we're keeping it fresh with delicate herbs, but many different flavourings would work with this preparation.

PREP

Fresh or frozen raspberries can be used. Pick the herb leaves off the stem, but don't worry about chopping them, as keeping them whole makes it easier to strain them.

EQUIPMENT

scale
measuring jug
peeler
saucepan
strainer

INGREDIENTS

500 g (4 cups) raspberries
250 g (9 oz) granulated white sugar
250 ml (1 cup) water
2 strips lemon peel
pinch salt
6 mint leaves
3 basil leaves

Try instead

This method can be used for most fruits. If layering in spices or harder herbs instead of delicate ones, add these at the beginning of the cooking process but taste regularly and remove if they become too prominent.

Pairs well with

This specific recipe pairs with vodka, contemporary gin, lighter rum and rye. However, switching out the basil and mint for other flavours can make it work with most spirits.

METHOD

Add everything except the herbs to your saucepan and stir over a low heat until combined. Simmer for about 20 minutes until reduced to a syrupy consistency. You don't want the raspberry to taste 'stewed' so don't cook it for too long. Take off the heat, remove the lemon peels, and add the mint and basil leaves to the syrup to infuse as it cools. Taste the syrup after an hour or two and, when the herbs are as pronounced as you would like, strain it off.

STORE

In the fridge for 1–2 weeks, or in the freezer for up to 3 months.

VANILLA AND EARL GREY SYRUP

Otherwise known as a London Fog, this flavour combination is straight up stolen from cafes, but, like many things in life, it's greatly improved by the addition of alcohol! This is an example of a cold infusion, so it's even less work than the other recipes in this section.

PREP

If you're using fresh vanilla beans, split them lengthways first, and bear in mind they can be used more than once (obviously with less potency), so allow them to dry then store them for another use. You can also use good-quality vanilla extract here, and the tea can be loose leaf or bags.

Try instead

This method can be used without the Earl Grey to make regular vanilla syrup, or without the vanilla to make any tea syrup. Vanilla also works well with chamomile, and Earl Grey works well with orange peel.

Pairs well with

Vodka, London Dry or contemporary gin, aged tequila, brandy, bourbon or blended whisky.

EQUIPMENT

measuring jug

scale

strainer

INGREDIENTS

300 ml (10 oz) boiling water

300 g (10½ oz) granulated white sugar

1 tablespoon loose-leaf Earl Grey tea, or 4 teabags

2 vanilla beans, split lengthways, or 1 teaspoon good-quality vanilla extract

METHOD

Add the boiling water to the sugar in a heatproof jug, then stir until combined. Add the tea and leave to steep for around 5 minutes. Strain the tea and add the vanilla. If you're using extract, simply stir until combined and you're done! If using beans, leave to infuse for at least 2 hours before straining.

STORE

In the fridge for 1 month, or in the freezer for up to 6 months.

SPICED HONEY OR AGAVE SYRUP

Here's a super simple little bonus recipe; I often just steep some herbs or spices in either honey or agave. Simply combine equal parts honey or agave with water over a low heat and add the flavourings of your choice for a minimal fuss flavour bomb.

PREP

If you're using ginger, for example, slice it first to give it more surface area for infusion, but most herbs and spices can just be popped in whole.

Try instead

Baking spices, spicy spices, hardy herbs – anything really!

Pairs well with

You can tailor this to suit most spirits, or just add hot water (and maybe a splash of whisky) for a ready-made hot toddy!

EQUIPMENT

measuring jug

peeler

saucepan

strainer

INGREDIENTS

250 ml (1 cup) honey or agave

250 ml (1 cup) water

(Suggested flavourings)

1 small knob ginger

2 strips orange peel

2 cinnamon sticks

METHOD

Add the honey or agave and water to a saucepan and stir until combined. Add your chosen flavourings and simmer for 5 minutes. Take off the heat and leave to cool fully before straining – the longer you leave it, the more pronounced the flavours will be.

STORE

In the fridge for 1 month, or in the freezer for up to 6 months.

OLEOS AND SHERBETS

Who says Latin is a dead language? Certainly not bartenders, who have resurrected the 'oleo saccharum' or 'oil sugar' method to add a citrusy zing to their drinks. Oleos form the basis of punch-style drinks. If you take it further and add fresh citrus juice to your oleo, this makes it a sherbet: essentially, a home-made sweet-and-sour mix. The sugar stabilises the juice, making it last longer than just freshly squeezed juice alone, and the added element of the citrus oil from the skins gives oleos and sherbets a wonderful intensity that brings the citrus to the forefront.

Tips and tricks for best results

+ Buy unwaxed citrus if you can, as we want the moisture to be able to leach out from the peel and dissolve the sugar.

+ Try to get as much white pith off your peel as possible to stop it becoming too bitter.

+ The oleo technique (see opposite) doesn't generate much volume, so bear that in mind when planning recipes. In punches, for instance, it is usually supplemented with other sweeteners, such as liqueurs, or you can lengthen it with juice to make a sherbet as mentioned, or with vinegar to make a shrub (see page 86).

+ Leaving the peel and sugar out at room temperature will speed up the process, but if that makes you nervous, it does work in the fridge, it might just take a little longer.

LEMON AND THYME OLEO

This is very much a recipe template; all manner of citrus and accent flavourings can be used.

PREP

Peel lemons and trim as much white pith off as possible. Thyme can be picked or left whole.

EQUIPMENT

peeler

scale

bowl or jar

muddler or wooden spoon

strainer

INGREDIENTS

peel of 5 lemons

2 thyme sprigs

200 g (7 oz) granulated white sugar, plus extra if needed to fully cover the peels

NOTE

You can keep the peels and dehydrate them in a food dehydrator or low oven then blitz them to make a candied lemon powder which can be used to garnish the rims of your glasses.

Try instead

Literally any other citrus will work in this recipe, and you can omit the thyme or experiment with other herbs or spices. I often like to mix citruses as well, for example, and it's a good way to experiment with more expensive or seasonal fruits, such as blood orange or yuzu, too.

Pairs well with

You can tailor this to suit most spirits, but this particular recipe works with vodka, London Dry or contemporary gin, lighter rum, blanco or aged tequila, mezcal, brandy and rye whiskey.

METHOD

Add the lemon peels, thyme and sugar to a bowl or jar and muddle (using a wooden spoon if you don't have a muddler or mortar) to start releasing the citrus oils. Cover and leave overnight, stirring (if in a bowl) or shaking (if in a jar) occasionally. Once the sugar has almost fully dissolved, give it a final stir and strain the peels (see Note) and thyme out. It will be thicker than a syrup – more of a sludge – but very potent. A little goes a long way.

STORE

In a sealed container in the fridge for up to 2 weeks.

CHILLI LIME SHERBET

The original Gimlet recipe was just gin and lime cordial, and this recipe puts a modern twist on this combination. Pair the bright lime with a little kick of chilli and your favourite spirit, and you'll have your new favourite 'two-ingredient' cocktail.

PREP

Peel the limes and trim as much white pith off as possible. If you're using fresh chilli, remove the seeds if you prefer it less spicy (or leave them in if you're feeling fiery!) and roughly chop. If you're nervous about heat, either leave the chillies whole or halve them so they can be easily removed during the process. Remember, though, that you will be lengthening the sherbet with juice, so the final product will be less intense than the sherbet.

NOTE

You can keep the peels and dehydrate them in a food dehydrator or low oven then blitz them to make a candied, spicy lime powder which can be used to garnish the rims of your glasses.

Try instead

Literally any other citrus, and you can omit the chilli or experiment with other herbs or spices as accent flavours.

Pairs well with

You can tailor this to suit most spirits, but this particular recipe works well with vodka, London Dry or contemporary gin, blanco or aged tequila, mezcal and lighter or heavier rum.

EQUIPMENT

peeler
juicer
scale
bowl or jar
muddler
strainer

INGREDIENTS

peel and juice of 6 limes

1 teaspoon chilli flakes or 1 red chilli, to taste

200 g (7 oz) granulated white sugar, plus extra if needed to ensure the peels are fully covered

METHOD

Add the lime peels, chilli and sugar to a bowl or jar and muddle to start releasing the citrus oils. Cover and leave overnight, stirring (if in a bowl) or shaking (if in a jar) occasionally. Once the sugar is almost fully dissolved, slowly add the lime juice while stirring to dissolve the rest of the sugar until it reaches a pourable syrup consistency. Strain the peels (see Note) and chilli out.

STORE

In a sealed container in the fridge for up to 2 weeks.

BANANA SKIN OLEO

While citrus is most commonly used for oleos, they're not the only fruit that contains delicious oils in their skin – bananas do too! This works perfectly well with just the peels, but you will get a more pronounced fruit flavour if you add some banana flesh as well. Just be gentle in your handling of them so the syrup doesn't get too cloudy.

PREP

Use ripe, but not overripe bananas. Peel, and then chop the peels into smaller pieces. Lightly smash the cinnamon sticks.

EQUIPMENT

scale

measuring jug

bowl or jar

strainer

INGREDIENTS

250 g (9 oz) banana peels (or however much you have available, just adjust the ingredients quantities up or down)

2 cinnamon sticks

250 g (9 oz) granulated white sugar (or brown sugar for a more intense flavour, but make sure it's not too soft as you need a bit of friction to pull the oils out)

100 ml (3½ oz) water, if needed

pinch salt

Try instead

Use other spices, herbs or nuts to complement the banana flavour.

Pairs well with

Lighter or heavier rums, blanco or aged tequila and bourbon.

METHOD

Add the banana peels and cinnamon sticks to a bowl or jar and cover with the sugar. Cover, shake or stir gently to combine and leave for at least 24 hours, preferably 48 hours. The resultant liquid can be quite thick, so add a little water if needed to loosen and make it pourable, then strain. Add a pinch of salt and stir to dissolve.

STORE

In a sealed container in the fridge for up to 2 weeks

SHRUBS

Shrubs are another awesome addition to your arsenal if you don't have fresh citrus around because they are essentially syrups spiked with vinegar, and they help hit two sides of the Taste Triangle simultaneously. This means they have a wonderful balance of both sweetness and acid, making them a bit of a one-stop-shop ingredient. You can make them with or without heat – the cold method is really just an extension of the oleo method detailed on the previous pages but using the whole fruit rather than just the pith and adding vinegar.

I often use these as a basis for non-alcoholic drinks; just topping them up with soda water (club soda) can create an elegant mocktail. Of course, a shot of something boozy in there works, too!

Tips and tricks for best results

+ Choose your vinegar wisely. Harsh distilled vinegars will only add harsh acid, and you want something a bit more delicate and nuanced for the best effect. A good-quality apple-cider vinegar works well in most situations, but you can also experiment with things like wine vinegars, or balsamic or flavoured fruit vinegars. Bottom line: if you wouldn't put it on your salad, don't put it in your shrub.

+ Control your temperature. Honestly, I find most shrubs benefit from little to no heat as you want them to be really bright and fresh, unless you are deliberately leaning into a richer, stewed flavour.

+ The vinegar can be added at multiple stages in the process so don't stress if you make it and it's not sharp enough. You can always add more vinegar at the end, so less is more in the beginning. You can even just add vinegar to a syrup you've already made if you decide it would benefit from some zing, or want it to last longer.

+ Try to prepare it in advance. The flavour of a shrub will mellow over time, so preparing it at least a day or two in advance – ideally up to a week – will make it a more rounded ingredient.

+ In properly sanitised, tightly sealed containers, shrubs will last a long time and don't even need to be refrigerated because of the preservation magic of the vinegar. That said, if you're opening it to use it often, it's best to keep it in the fridge to be safe and try to consume it within 3 months for optimum flavour, but they should last longer.

BLUEBERRY AND LEMONGRASS SHRUB

I like this method of preparation for blueberries in particular as they are quite a delicate fruit and a shrub really lets them shine. That said, this recipe is a basic blueprint for any cold-process, fruit-and-accent-flavour shrub so feel free to mix it up!

PREP

You can use fresh or frozen blueberries. I actually find frozen can help the process as they release even more moisture as they defrost. Give the lemongrass a bash (you can use a muddler or a rolling pin, or just bend it a few times) to get the juices flowing, then roughly chop it into 5 cm (2 in) lengths.

NOTE

I like to remove some whole fruit at this point, as they are essentially candied, and can make a nice garnish.

Try instead

Any high moisture-content fruit including berries, orchard fruit, stone fruit, and some tropical fruit, such as pineapple, melon and mango. Then you can experiment with flavour friend accents.

Pairs well with

This specific recipe pairs well with vodka, contemporary gin, lighter rum and blanco tequila. However, switching out the flavours can make it work with anything!

EQUIPMENT

scale
measuring jug
bowl or jar
strainer

INGREDIENTS

500 g (1 lb 2 oz) blueberries

2 lemongrass stalks, bruised

250 g (9 oz) granulated white sugar

250 ml (1 cup) apple-cider vinegar

METHOD

Add the blueberries, lemongrass and sugar to your bowl or jar and give it a stir. Cover and leave in the fridge overnight. The juice from the fruit should release and start to dissolve the sugar (essentially, you're making an oleo in this step, see page 78). Stir until the sugar is fully dissolved and then strain (see Note). Gently press the rest to remove as much liquid as possible. Pour the vinegar into the blueberry mixture. You can do this in stages and taste as you go until you get the right balance of sweetness and acidity for you.

STORE

In a sealed container in the fridge for up to 6 months.

MANDARIN AND PINK PEPPER SHRUB

Using every part of a citrus fruit – the peel, flesh and juice – creates
a really rounded flavour and a more nuanced result in a shrub.
The floral spice of pink peppercorns works so well with mandarin,
but of course you can switch this out for another sweet spice if you
can't find any.

PREP

Peel the mandarins (reserving
the peel) and break the fruit into
segments. If you want to use the
segments for garnish, 'butterfly'
them by cutting along the longer
side, leaving the membrane
intact, and gently opening each
segment out into a butterfly
shape. Otherwise just roughly cut
the segments in half. Gently bash
the peppercorns. If you have a
juicer that can juice mandarins,
use fresh juice. Otherwise, you
can buy it, or just use orange juice
if you can't find any.

EQUIPMENT

scale

measuring jug

bowl or jar

strainer

INGREDIENTS

500 g (1 lb 2 oz) peeled
mandarins and their skins
(about 6 mandarins)

200 ml (7 oz) mandarin or
orange juice

2 teaspoons pink peppercorns

250 g (9 oz) granulated
white sugar

250 ml (1 cup) Champagne or
white-wine vinegar

NOTE

*If you decided to 'butterfly' the
mandarin segments, dehydrate
them in a food dehydrator or
a low oven for a really cute
garnish. Just be gentle with
your stirring and straining to
keep them intact.*

Try instead

All other citrus fruits work well
with this method, with flavour
accents of your choice.

Pairs well with

Vodka, contemporary gin, lighter
rum, blanco tequila, mezcal and
bourbon. I also love this with
dry sherry.

METHOD

Add the mandarin peels and segments, peppercorns and sugar
to your bowl or jar and give it a stir. Cover and leave in the fridge
overnight. Stir and add juice to dissolve all the sugar, then strain
(see Note). Add the Champagne or vinegar in stages, tasting as you
go until you get the right balance of sweetness and acidity for you.

STORE

In a sealed container in the fridge for up to 6 months.

BALSAMIC FIG SHRUB

While I more often use the cold method (see pages 89 and 90) when making shrubs, it can be fun to lean into a slightly more 'cooked' flavour profile to make a richer shrub that stands up well to darker spirits.

PREP

You can use fresh or dried figs for this. If you're using fresh, just cook them a little longer, or you might prefer to use the cold method (see page 89). Keep the thyme sprigs whole.

EQUIPMENT

scale

measuring jug

saucepan

strainer

INGREDIENTS

250 g (9 oz) demerara sugar, plus extra if needed (or use granulated white sugar, but the demerara suits the heavier flavour profile we're going for here)

150 ml (5 oz) balsamic vinegar, plus extra if needed

100 ml (3½ oz) apple-cider vinegar, plus extra if needed

500 g (1 lb 2 oz) figs

5 thyme sprigs

pinch salt

NOTE

Remove the thyme sprigs and keep the solids as it is quite delicious in its own right. Try it on ice cream!

Try instead

This is a good method for all dried fruit: prunes, dried apricots, etc. Otherwise, anything that lends itself to a more stewed flavour, such as rhubarb, apples or pears, will also work well.

Pairs well with

Aged tequila, heavier rum, brandy and whiskies.

METHOD

Gently heat the sugar and vinegars in a saucepan until the sugar dissolves. You can use all balsamic if you like a more pronounced flavour, but I like to use two different vinegars for a subtler flavour. Add the figs, thyme and salt and simmer over a low heat for 15 minutes for dried figs, or 20 minutes for fresh figs. Don't allow the mixture to reduce by too much, but you can lengthen it with some water if it gets too thick. Allow to cool, then strain, gently pressing to extract as much liquid as possible (see Note). Taste and add more sugar or vinegar if necessary to balance the flavour.

STORE

In a sealed container in the fridge for up to 6 months.

PUREES AND PRESERVES

Pureeing is essentially a cheat's way of circumventing the labour-intensive work of muddling. You could, for example, muddle strawberries for something like a Daiquiri, or you could blitz up some strawberries with sugar and use that instead of the simple syrup. Purees also usually retain more of the original fruit's freshness and texture as opposed to syrups, for example, which are subtler.

I'm using the term 'preserves' here to cover jams, jellies, compôtes, marmalades, chutneys and any other cooked fruit and sugar combination you can think of. The lines between these ingredients are often blurred, and as long as the result is delicious, it doesn't really matter what you call them!

Preserves generally lean towards the sweet side of the Taste Triangle, but retaining the natural acid in the fruit or loading them up with added citrus and spice can help add a little sourness and bitterness to the mix as well.

Tips and tricks for best results

+ Purees rely mostly on the natural sweetness of the fruit, which is great, but this means they don't contain much sugar or acid to help preserve them. Adding some powdered ascorbic or citric acid can help preserve their colour and freshness, but they should be used or frozen quite quickly regardless.

+ Preserves rely on pectin for their thicker texture. This occurs naturally in a lot of fruits to a greater or lesser extent, especially in the seeds and skins. You can also buy pectin as an additive. However, for the purpose of cocktails, it's not that big a deal if your preserve is a little runny because it's going to be shaken up and strained anyway! Just call it a compôte and be done with it, as long as the flavour is there.

+ That said, bringing your preserve to a proper boil is important to help release natural pectin from the fruit. Normally I'm an advocate of low-and-slow cooking, but this stage is necessary in this instance. That said, don't overdo it. You don't want to lose all the freshness from your ingredient and it's easier to deal with undersetting than oversetting.

+ If you want to aim for properly shelf-stable preserves, sterilisation of your jars or bottles is very important (wash jars and lids in hot and soapy water and dry fully in a low oven). You also need to fill the jars to the brim and seal the lids tightly while the mixture is still hot to create a proper seal. Honestly, I usually open them too soon after making them to justify the faff and store them more like syrups in the fridge. If you have more patience than me there are a lot of great resources for proper jarring procedures online.

PEAR AND CHAMOMILE PUREE

At Bomba, the bar I managed for many years, one of the best-selling drinks is the 'Bomba Bellini'. The original Bellini is made with peach puree and prosecco and is, of course, delicious, but they've taken that template and switched it up with more seasonal fruit purees, and often with another flavour layered in there as well. It's a perfect example of the premise of this book: using seasonal and affordable ingredients to put a spin on your drinks. This recipe is one of my favourite versions of puree to use in the Bellini format (see page 140).

PREP

If you're using fresh pears, wait until they are properly ripe or poach them lightly beforehand so they are soft enough to blend easily. Peel, core and chop them roughly. Otherwise, you can use tinned pears, but look for ones in juice rather than syrup (or replace the sugar in the recipe with syrup from the tin to taste; you won't need much as the pear flesh will already be sweet). Brew the chamomile tea according to the packet instructions. You can use either loose leaf or a teabag, just remove it before blending. Warm the honey slightly so it is pourable.

Try instead

Peaches or apples fit easily into this recipe with the honey and chamomile, but we switch it up with all sorts of seasonal fruit and matching accent flavours throughout the year.

Pairs well with

Sparkling wine! But also vodka, London Dry or contemporary gin, lighter rum, blanco tequila, brandy and whiskies.

EQUIPMENT

scale

measuring jug

kettle or saucepan

blender

INGREDIENTS

500 g (1 lb 2 oz) pears

100 ml (3½ oz) honey, to taste (try to use a lighter-flavoured honey, or use half regular honey half sugar if you don't want the honey flavour to take over)

100 ml (3½ oz) brewed chamomile tea

pinch salt

½ teaspoon ascorbic or citric acid (optional; see page 96)

METHOD

Add everything to the blender and blitz until smooth. The puree will be thicker than a syrup or a shrub but should still be pourable. You can add the tea in stages, if you like, to make sure you achieve the desired texture.

STORE

In a sealed container in the fridge for a week, or in the freezer for up to 3 months.

SPICED CUMQUAT MARMALADE

Despite my fiancé being an extremely dedicated plant dad, the only one of our fruit trees that produces fruit with any regularity is our cumquat tree. Being the bitter little things they are, cumquats are not quite as versatile as most other citrus fruits. So, when life gives you cumquats, make marmalade! In full disclosure, this is a slapdash bartender version but it works perfectly well for the purpose and is much less fuss than most versions, but still delicious!

PREP

Quarter or slice the cumquats (depending on size). Don't worry about the pips; just strain any drinks you use the marmalade in before serving. You can cover the cumquats with the water and leave to soak overnight if you have time. This softens the fruit, which helps it to cook faster and keep the flavour fresher, but it's not imperative. If you do this, cook the cumquats in the same water you soaked them in.

Try instead

Any other citrus. Spices can be switched up or left out entirely. If you're using whole spices or slices of something, like ginger, pick them out before storing.

Pairs well with

Vodka, lighter or heavier rum, aged tequila, mezcal, brandy and whiskies.

EQUIPMENT

scale
measuring jug
microplane
juicer
saucepan

INGREDIENTS

500 g (1 lb 2 oz) cumquats

250 ml (1 cup) water, or enough to cover the cumquats

250 g (9 oz) granulated white sugar, or to taste (I like to keep my marmalade quite tart, but you can definitely add more sugar if you prefer)

pinch salt

1 teaspoon ground cumin

½ teaspoon smoked paprika

zest and juice of ½ lemon

METHOD

Put the cumquats, water and sugar in a saucepan and stir over a low heat for 10–15 minutes until the fruit is tender and the sugar has dissolved. Add the salt, spices and lemon zest and juice while still over a low heat, then increase the heat and bring to a rolling boil. Reduce the heat to medium and continue boiling for about 20 minutes, or until the marmalade has thickened. To check if it has reached setting point place a small plate in the freezer until cold, then drop a dollop of marmalade on the cold plate. Tilt the plate and if the marmalade doesn't run, you're good to go. If it does, continue boiling until it does set on the plate. Or you can just eyeball it if you're a cowboy like me. Fish out any pips you can see.

STORE

Properly jarred and sealed in jars in the pantry for up to 6 months. Once opened, refrigerate and use within 3 months.

RHUBARB AND FENNEL JAM

Rhubarb is a great vegetable to use when making jam as its natural tartness means it can take a fair amount of sugar and cooking and still taste vibrant. In fact, my Scottish granny used to keep me quiet as a kid by giving me a stick of rhubarb and a bag of sugar. You'd dip the rhubarb in the sugar then gnaw away on it, so this recipe takes me right back to her kitchen. Fennel is a great bridging flavour; it has enough anise for sweetness but with a beguiling savoury edge.

PREP

If you have fresh fennel and the time, roughly chop the fronds (keeping them quite large), cover in the sugar and leave overnight. The scent of the fennel will infuse the sugar and help the flavour carry more, and you can scoop out the fennel whenever you feel the flavour is right. Otherwise, fennel seeds are a great replacement, but just add them with everything else.

Try instead
Plum and fennel is another great flavour combination, as is rhubarb and ginger. You could also add another fruit, like strawberries, to this recipe.

Pairs well with
Vodka, London Dry or contemporary gin, lighter rum, blanco tequila and mezcal.

EQUIPMENT

scale
measuring jug
microplane
juicer
large bowl
saucepan

INGREDIENTS

500 g (1 lb 2 oz) chopped rhubarb

fronds of 1 small fennel bulb, or 1½ teaspoons fennel seeds

250 ml (1 cup) water

250 g (9 oz) granulated white sugar, or to taste

zest, juice and husks (including any seeds) of 1 orange

pinch salt

METHOD

If you're using the fennel-scented sugar (see Prep), I usually remove all but a couple of fronds before adding the sugar as I prefer a lighter fennel flavour. Add all the ingredients to a large bowl, including the husks and seeds of the orange, as these contain pectin, which will help the jam set. Cover and leave for at least 1 hour, or for up to 12 hours. Scoop out the husks and seeds before transferring the mixture to a saucepan. Alternatively, just stick all the ingredients straight in the saucepan and cook. It will still taste great, but it might not be the ideal texture. Cook over a low heat for about 15 minutes, then remove any remaining fennel fronds. Bring to a rolling boil then reduce the heat to medium and continue boiling for about 20 minutes, or until the rhubarb has broken down and thickened. To check if it has reached setting point place a small plate in the freezer until cold, then drop a dollop of jam on the cold plate. Tilt the plate and if the jam doesn't run, you're good to go. If it does, continue boiling until it reaches setting point.

STORE

Properly jarred and sealed in the pantry for up to 6 months. Once opened, refrigerate and use within 3 months.

INFUSIONS AND
FAT-WASHING

Whether you want to highlight your favourite flavours in one bottle or hide the inadequacies of another, using an infusion or fat wash is a (relatively) easy way to customise your creations by altering the alcoholic components of an ingredient, or the 'strong' part of the Taste Triangle.

Infusions use a solvent (alcohol) to extract flavour and aromatic compounds from ingredients. Or, as I like to explain it, sticking sh*t in a bottle and hoping it tastes good! Fat-washing is a little more complicated, but not much; you're essentially just adding a fatty substance, such as butter or oil, to alcohol then freezing it to remove the fatty solids, leaving dissolved flavour compounds and an altered texture behind.

Tips and tricks for best results

+ Different flavourings will infuse at different speeds – sometimes only a day is needed, sometimes up to a week – so taste your infusion each day until it reaches your desired intensity. Over-extraction can happen, where flavours turn bitter or muddy, so watch out for any sign of that and strain immediately.

+ In this section I've provided recipes for a standard 700 ml (23½ oz) bottle, but I'd recommend starting on a smaller scale when experimenting with new flavour combinations.

+ While a higher alcohol content (such as that in a spirit) will speed up infusion, it does still work in lower-ABV products like sherry or vermouth. It just happens a little more gently, but that actually suits more delicate fruits and herbs anyway.

+ Increased surface area will affect the speed of infusion, too, but this is helpful in controlling the outcome. Chilli, for example, is a strong flavour that infuses quickly, but if you wanted to pair it with a lighter flavour like cucumber you could leave the chilli whole and slice the cucumber thinly and that will help to sync them up.

+ For fat-washing, use less of stronger-flavoured fats like bacon fat or sesame oil, and more of neutral-flavoured fats like olive oil or coconut oil.

+ If solids are all fully strained out after infusing, then the infused spirit can be stored at room temperature out of direct sunlight and not in the fridge. (Anything wine based should be refrigerated once opened whether infused or not, of course.) Fat-washed spirits need to be refrigerated if not being used within a few days in case they're not fully filtered and the fat goes rancid.

STRAWBERRY AND TARRAGON FINO SHERRY

For me, fino sherry is a wonderful balance of fruity and herbaceous, so dialling those elements up to eleven by infusing it with fruit (strawberry) and herbs (tarragon) just makes sense and helps the sherry have a more pronounced presence in drinks, making it a great base for lower-ABV options.

PREP

Hull and slice or chop the strawberries quite small and leave the fresh tarragon whole.

Try instead

Delicate and floral fruits like peach, pear or apricot, paired with grassy and fresh herbs like dill, sage or mint.

Pairs well with

As a solo base, or with vodka, contemporary gin, blanco tequila and lighter rum.

EQUIPMENT

measuring jug

airtight container, jar or bottle

strainer

METHOD

Add the strawberries, tarragon (if using fresh) and sherry to your container, seal and refrigerate. If using dried tarragon, add after 24 hours. Check the flavour at 48 hours. I generally like it around this point as the flavour is identifiable but still delicate. You can take it further, but I would remove any fresh tarragon at this point as it can start to taste a bit less fresh. Once you're happy with the intensity of the flavour, strain it off. Definitely don't keep the strawberries for garnish – they're disgusting at this point, I can tell you from experience.

STORE

In a sealed container in the fridge for around 1 month.

INGREDIENTS

7 strawberries

3–4 fresh tarragon sprigs or 2 teaspoons dried tarragon

700 ml (23½ oz) fino sherry

ORANGE AND CHILLI VODKA

Vodka, of course, is the easiest canvas for infusions, and my choice of flavours here is entirely arbitrary, as any complementary ingredients can work against this fairly neutral backdrop. Try the Devil's Advocate on page 163; it's an absolute banger.

PREP

Peel the orange in large strips and remove excess pith. Slice the chillies in half and remove the seeds if you prefer, although I like to keep them in for this one.

Try instead

Pretty much anything can be infused in vodka!

Pairs well with

These flavours also infuse well in blanco tequila or lighter rum. Use in cocktails with baking spice and citrus flavours.

EQUIPMENT

peeler

airtight container, jar or bottle

strainer

INGREDIENTS

700 ml (23½ oz) vodka

peel of ½ orange (approx. 3–4 strips)

2 red chillies

METHOD

Add everything to your container, seal and store in a cool, dark place for 1–2 days. Both orange and chilli are quite bold flavours which will infuse in vodka easily, so leaving them in larger pieces means you can pull one or the other out if the flavour starts to become overwhelming. It really depends on how spicy the chillies are. Generally speaking, I've found that 48 hours is the sweet spot for this infusion, but taste and see. You can definitely leave it longer – if you dare.

STORE

In a sealed container in a cool dark place for up to 1 year.

DIY SPICED RUM

I often find spiced rum too sweet, especially when trying to balance it in cocktails as the 'strong' component alongside other sweet elements. So, why not make your own with sweeter-style spices but no added sugar? You want a decent quality but not overly distinctive rum for this as anything too funky will fight with the other flavours.

PREP

Peel and slice the ginger, grate the nutmeg and split the vanilla bean lengthways. Peel the orange and remove any excess pith.

EQUIPMENT

peeler

microplane

airtight container, jar or bottle

strainer

INGREDIENTS

700 ml (23½ oz) heavier rum

2 large strips orange peel

1 cinnamon stick

1 star anise

6 allspice berries

6 coffee beans

1 vanilla bean

2.5 cm (1 in) piece ginger

¼ teaspoon grated nutmeg

Try instead

Tailor the spice profile to your own liking. You could make it more savoury by removing the vanilla and using cardamom and peppercorn, or focus the flavour more by concentrating on one or two key flavours and upping the amount used. I've also leaned into the fresher flavour of lighter rum by using a tropical fruit such as pineapple or mango alongside cinnamon and ginger. Or try adding apple and similar spices to bourbon for an apple-pie spiced whiskey.

Pairs well with

Use in cocktails with tropical or stone fruit flavours.

METHOD

Add everything to your container, seal and store in a cool, dark place for 1–2 days. Taste every 24 hours until the flavours are to your liking. I usually pull the vanilla out early as I don't like it to be an overly prominent flavour. Strain when you're happy with the profile and intensity. Again, around 48 hours is usually enough to give this a nice gentle spice, but you can take it longer for a stronger flavour if you prefer.

STORE

In a sealed container a cool dark place for up to 1 year.

COCONUT FAT-WASHED CAMPARI

Fat-washing burst onto the bar scene by way of a bacon fat-washed bourbon Old Fashioned from New York's Please Don't Tell, and the bar world hasn't looked back since. It certainly works well with richer fats and heavier spirits (I love a brown butter-washed rum or whisk(e)y), but this technique is very versatile. Here, coconut oil puts a sweet and nutty spin on our favourite red aperitif.

PREP

Warm coconut oil over a low heat until melted.

Try instead

You can use this method on all manner of spirits and fats: butter, olive oil, sesame oil or even cheese can be used on anything from vodka to whisk(e)y. You can add other flavours as well with fruits, vegetables or spices as you are melting the fat.

Pairs well with

Take your Negroni on an exotic vacation or bring a bitter twist to tropical drinks.

EQUIPMENT

scale

saucepan

freezer-safe airtight container

strainer and/or muslin (cheesecloth) or a coffee filter

INGREDIENTS

150 g (5½ oz) coconut oil (about 9 tablespoons)

700 ml (23½ oz) Campari or other bitter red aperitif

METHOD

Add the melted coconut oil to the Campari in a freezer-safe container, mix and leave at room temperature for about 2 hours to allow the flavour to infuse. Seal and transfer to the freezer overnight. When you pull it out, the oil should have solidified at the top of the mixture. Skim it off then strain to remove any smaller particles. The finer the strainer you use – such as a piece of muslin (cheesecloth) or a coffee filter – the more fat particles you will take out. This helps achieve a clearer but less textural final result, so decide whether aesthetics or viscosity are more important for your drink recipe.

STORE

In a sealed container in the fridge for up to 6 months.

PEANUT BUTTER BOURBON

Peanut butter is a great option for fat-washing as it adds both texture and flavour.

PREP

Make sure the peanut butter is at room temperature or even slightly warmed to make it easier to work with.

EQUIPMENT

scale

baking tray or other flat storage option

strainer

coffee filter

sealable, freezer-safe container (optional)

INGREDIENTS

700 ml (23½ oz) bourbon

250 g (9 oz) peanut butter (try to use a natural, unsalted peanut butter. A smooth one will make it easier to strain)

NOTE

Unfortunately, you do lose some volume of the spirit with this method as it absorbs into the peanut butter. You could also try turning it into a peanut butter brittle!

Try instead

This works well with other dark spirits such as a heavier rum or blended whisk(e)y.

Pairs well with

The peanut butter is quite a strong flavour, so I tend to keep this pretty simple in Old Fashioned or Manhattan-style drinks – try it with some cacao bitters for a sweet treat.

METHOD

There are two options here: if you want minimal mess, you can wrap the peanut butter in a coffee filter and use it almost as a teabag in the bourbon. It does take longer to infuse this way (about 48 hours) and the flavour isn't quite as pronounced. Or, for maximum flavour extraction, spread the peanut butter on a baking tray to increase the surface area and pour the bourbon on top. Wrap tightly and leave overnight, then strain through a coffee filter (you may need more than one filter to complete the straining if the filter gets clogged with solids). If your liquid is still a little cloudy and oily after this – and you want it to be perfectly clear – you can put it in the freezer overnight and skim extra particles off the top, and even strain again. Personally, I don't mind it being a little cloudy as it's all just flavour, baby!

STORE

In a sealed container in the fridge for up to 6 months.

COCKTAIL BITTERS AND TINCTURES

These are really just an extension of the infusions in the previous chapter, but in a much more concentrated format to be used as drops and dashes to season your cocktails. The only real difference between the two is that bitters have, well, a pronounced bitterness, whereas tinctures are just intense – not necessarily bitter – infusions. Both tend to add sour or bitter to your drinks through fruit and spice.

While I dabble in making these myself, there's a little more to it than your usual recipe, so I've enlisted the help of my friend Jake Taylor, co-founder of Mister Bitters (my favourite local bitters brand) to give you tip-top advice on this technique.

Jake's tips and tricks for best results

+ For your base spirit, you want something as neutral as possible with a fairly high ABV. We (Mister Bitters) started out with 40 per cent vodka, which is fine, but 50 per cent vodka is even better! You can experiment with different base spirits if you want, but you really need something that will allow the botanicals to shine, such as vodka or a lightly flavoured rum. Try to avoid really high (95 per cent) ABV spirits to get the best flavour extraction – between 45–60 per cent is ideal.

+ Start small. It's easy to manage infusions in small amounts as it's less of a stress when they don't work! It also means you have less wastage of spirit and you can try more things. Be precise with your measurements; consistency enables you to repeat your infusions and improve them more easily and efficiently.

+ I would recommend starting with single-botanical infusions. This will essentially give you a bunch of single flavours to blend together, like a cocktail. Once you know how your botanicals behave then you can move on to one-pot infusions.

+ Taste regularly. I suggest tasting every week at the beginning and then every day when it's close to being ready. Generally it takes about a month to properly infuse, except for really intense flavours or high-concentration infusions.

+ Really full-on botanicals, such as very hot chillies, can be tricky, so be sparing with them. Conversely, ingredients with a high water content are often pretty light in flavour and they can dilute your bitters, slowing the rate of infusion and leaving you with a weaker flavour and ABV – think fruit flesh or fresh leaves. I have also never had any luck with pineapple; it just goes funky too quickly!

+ Filter properly to get the correct flavour and texture in the finished product – muslin (cheesecloth) or a coffee filter works well.

NOTE

Specialist bittering agents such as wormwood, gentian, angelica root, cinchona (see below) and cassia bark tend to be the backbone of most commercial bitters, but can be hard to find. You can search them out and experiment, of course, or rely on more common ingredients with a bitter edge, as I have here, like coffee, cacao, citrus peels and some spices. I also like using black teas and nuts.

*Please be aware the cinchona bark contains quinine, which you may recognise as a key ingredient in tonic water, but which can also be poisonous in larger quantities. There are guidelines online around a safe amount to use – cocktailsafe.org is a great resource if you're ever unsure about an ingredient you're using, but if in doubt, steer clear.

INDIVIDUAL TINCTURE

Following Jake's advice of making individual infusions rather than an all-in-one, I thought it would be more useful to include the general method for all infusions, and then suggest some combinations.

PREP

Using whole botanicals rather than powdered will make the final product easier to strain, but be sure to give them a quick bash before using to increase the surface area. Peel any citrus and remove any pith. Clean and trim any fruit or vegetables (but don't stress about removing the skin; this is where a lot of the bitter flavour lives), and roughly chop. Nuts work best toasted and teas should be loose leaf. A general-rule ratio for any infusion is one-part fresh botanical to two-parts alcohol, or one-part dried botanical to five-parts alcohol. Once blended, there is the option to dilute with water and/or lightly sweeten with sugar, honey or maple syrup (see opposite).

EQUIPMENT

measuring jug

scale

airtight container, jar or bottle

fine-mesh sieve and muslin (cheesecloth) or coffee filter, for straining

saucepan

dropper or pipette, for blending

small dropper or dasher bottle

INGREDIENTS

1-part fresh botanical, such as fruit and fresh herbs, to 2-parts alcohol, something neutral such as vodka

1-part dried botanical, such as barks and spices, to 5-parts alcohol, something neutral such as vodka

METHOD

Add your chosen botanical to your container, then add the alcohol. Seal, shake well and store in a cool, dark place for about 1 month. Check periodically (put a drop or two on your hands to smell and add a drop or two to a small amount of water to taste. You can taste it straight, but it will be quite full-on!). Start by checking once a week, then every day once you start to smell and taste the botanical character becoming more pronounced than the alcohol. Shake as often as you remember (ideally once a day, but let's be realistic here). Don't be afraid to let the flavour get very strong – unlike in the infusions section – as these bitters will be used in very small quantities, but watch out for any indication of the flavour becoming unpleasant. Strain thoroughly when you're happy with it, once through a fine-mesh sieve and once through a piece of muslin (cheesecloth) or a coffee filter.

If you want to dilute your bitters with water but keep the intensity of flavour, retain the botanicals after straining and cover with water in a saucepan. Bring to the boil and allow to simmer for about 10 minutes, then remove from the heat and leave to cool. Put in a sealed container in a cool, dark place for 1 week before straining as above. This flavoured water can be used to dilute the alcohol.

Once you have a few of these tinctures, you can start experimenting with combining them. Start with literally a drop or two of each and see how they interact, then take it from there. You can sweeten it a little if you feel it is necessary, but again remember the volume and purpose of the bitters in the cocktail; they don't have to be entirely 'balanced' themselves. To level up the flavour, you can cover the same botanical in sugar and make an oleo, and add that, or use something like honey, agave or maple syrup to complement the flavour.

STORE

In small dropper or dasher bottles in a cool, dry place for up to 1 year.

ORANGE AND COFFEE BITTERS

Combining a warm citrus note with roasted, slightly bitter coffee beans gives a great twist on classic orange bitters. It's really versatile; it can be used in crisp and citrusy cocktails for depth, or with tropical flavours and darker spirits.

PREP

Prepare individual tinctures as on page 116. Go for whole coffee beans with a medium-to-dark roast.

Try instead

A brighter orange bitters with green cardamom and coriander seeds, or lean into the coffee more by lowering the proportion of orange and adding allspice.

Pairs well with

Vodka, London Dry gin, blanco or aged tequila, lighter or darker rums, brandy and whiskies.

EQUIPMENT

dropper or pipette, for blending
measuring jug
small dropper or dasher bottle

METHOD

Combine the tinctures in the ratio above, but feel free to taste and adjust to your preference. Sweeten with maple syrup, drop by drop, if you like.

STORE

In a small dropper or dasher bottle in a cool, dry place for up to 1 year.

INGREDIENTS

6-parts orange tincture
4-parts coffee tincture
1-part cacao nib tincture
1-part cinnamon tincture
maple syrup (optional), to taste

MANGO AND BLACK TEA BITTERS

Fruit and spice really are all things nice. Here, the black tea provides the bitter backbone to the tropical mango and warm, zingy spices.

PREP

Prepare individual tinctures as on page 116.

EQUIPMENT

dropper or pipette, for blending

measuring jug

small dropper or dasher bottle

INGREDIENTS

6-parts mango tincture

2-parts English Breakfast tea tincture

1-part ginger tincture

½-part cumin seed tincture

agave syrup (optional), to taste

Try instead

Try switching out the accent flavours. Chilli works well here, as does cardamom.

Pairs well with

Vodka, blanco or aged tequila, lighter or darker rum, brandy and whiskies.

METHOD

Combine the tinctures in the ratio above, but feel free to taste and adjust to your preference. Sweeten with agave syrup, drop by drop, if you like.

STORE

In a small dropper or dasher bottle in a cool, dry place for up to 1 year.

CHILLI TINCTURE

Having a chilli tincture on hand means you can spice up your life whenever you need to! You can use this in cooking, too. This one I tend to do all together as a one-pot infusion and just keep an eye on it until it reaches my desired spice level.

PREP

Halve the chillies and deseed if you prefer – I usually live life on the edge and leave them in, but I have a pretty high spice tolerance for a Scottish lass! Peel the limes and remove any excess pith. Toast the cashew nuts.

Try instead
You can tailor the accent flavours to the chillies used. Lime works really well with jalapeño, whereas orange works well with chipotle.

Pairs well with
Vodka, blanco or aged tequila, mezcal, lighter or darker rums.

EQUIPMENT

peeler

measuring jug

scale

airtight container, jar or bottle

fine-mesh sieve, muslin (cheesecloth) or a coffee filter, for straining

INGREDIENTS

1-part mixture of chillies (simple Thai red chillies and jalapeño, or experiment with ancho, habanero, cayenne, or chipotle – whatever spicy bois you can find!) to 2-parts alcohol

peel of ½ lime

toasted cashew nuts (optional; I find these tie the flavours together nicely, but you can leave them out if you're worried about nut allergies, or use cacao nibs or coffee beans instead)

honey (optional), to taste

METHOD

Add everything to your container and shake well. Leave in a cool dark place and check daily – this one usually only takes 3–7 days. Once you're happy with the flavour, strain well. Dilute and or/ sweeten with honey, if you like.

STORE

In a small dropper or dasher bottle in a cool, dry place for up to 1 year.

PICKLES AND FERMENTS

Both pickling and fermenting are venerable preservation methods that yield a similar, tangy result, but the processes are different. To put it very simply, in pickling you use an acidic brine (usually vinegar based) to preserve, whereas in fermentation bacteria converts the starches and sugars in the food to acids, gases and/or alcohol, and it becomes more stable that way. The process of converting complex molecules into simpler sugars and amino acids makes them taste better, and they become easier to digest, more nutritious and delicious. There is some crossover in that pickles can be lacto-fermented, but the most common method is a 'quick pickle' with no fermentation. Both are great ways to bring sourness, umami and depth to cocktails.

Being perfectly honest, I'm quite impatient, and pickling is quicker, so I tend to do more of that. Pickled garnishes are great, too, as they last longer and have less wastage than fresh while still adding another flavour dimension to a drink. The brine can also be used in a similar way to bitters: in small quantities to add a bright zing and an umami edge to drinks. While pickles do contain some sugar, they should be intense, acidic and salty, which is where they differ from shrubs, which are a sweeter and more rounded ingredient that can be used in larger quantities.

Fermentation, while a lengthier and more involved process, achieves an unparalleled depth of flavour and texture, so I've recruited the help of my friend and self-proclaimed fermentation nerd, Melbourne bartender Kayla Saito for some advice on flawless fermentation. So, what fermentation methods does Kayla recommend exploring for use in drinks?

Ferments in the bar

+ Fruit wine fermentation: yeast can ferment any fruit into wine by converting the sugar to alcohol. This is a great way to reduce waste; even pulp from juicing can be fermented by adding yeast, sugar and water. These wines can be used as a basis for home-made vermouths and liqueurs.

+ Lacto-fermentation: if you've been at a trendy bar recently you may well have seen a reference to this. It is traditionally used as a preservation method, so can be used to preserve produce at the height of its season. The process uses lactic-acid-producing bacteria and yeasts to convert sugar into lactic acid (an acid found in milk), and sometimes alcohol or carbon dioxide, in an oxygen-free environment. Salt is an important part of this method as it creates an ideal environment for the all-important bacteria, lactobacillus, to thrive.

+ Koji fermentation: koji is a strain of fungus, and this type of ferment is used in a lot of delicious things like sake, miso and soy sauce – umami, baby! Like yeast, koji kickstarts the fermentation process and turns starches and proteins into amino acids and sugars. Different strains of koji can be used for different results. Kayla recommends making shio koji by combining koji rice with salt and water and fermenting for a crumbly, flavour-packed paste that can be used as a salt substitute in cooking and drinks-making.

+ Kombucha and water kefirs: for these, a SCOBY (symbiotic culture of bacteria and yeast) is used to ferment tea or fruit and water to create a lightly sparkling, tangy drink that can be enjoyed alone or as part of a cocktail.

Kayla's tips and tricks for best results

+ When making either pickles or ferments, make sure all your equipment and your hands are well sanitised. You might even want to wear gloves; we want good bacteria to grow, not bad!

+ The salt is also important for both methods. You want to use a mineral-rich, natural salt rather than table salt which contains other ingredients such as iodine.

+ For pickling, use firmer fruit or vegetables. The pickling process softens the fruit, so if they are already very ripe you may end up with mush!

+ All ferments are different, so do your research. Some methods, like lacto-fermenting, take place in an oxygen-free environment whereas some, like kombucha, need to breathe so are done 'open air'.

+ Ferments are generally sensitive to temperature: too cool and the ferment might not take (so don't try and ferment in the fridge), too warm and you can lose control of the ferment. Room temperature in a dark place is usually good.

+ Keep an eye on your ferments. Fermenting done in an oxygen-free environment will still produce carbon dioxide, for example, so you need to make sure the pressure doesn't build too much by opening the jar daily to release the gas – explosions are never fun! If you're planning on doing a lot of fermenting, investing in an airlock is smart.

Here I have kept to a simple pickle recipe and a simple lacto-ferment recipe which can be applied to all sorts of different produce. To delve into other ferments, some more complicated equipment and ingredients are needed (airlocks, yeasts, SCOBYs, etc.), but these you should be able to throw together with whatever equipment you have on hand.

PICKLED MELON BALLS

These make a really pretty garnish, and the sweet, sour and spicy brine can be used in lots of different styles of drinks for a fruity and zesty pop. A melon baller will help here for aesthetics, but if you don't have one just chop the melon into dainty cubes; smaller pieces also mean they will pickle more quickly. This basic process can be used for all sorts of fruits and veggies.

PREP

Use a melon baller to scoop out the flesh of your melon. Chop the mint roughly. Peel and roughly slice the ginger.

EQUIPMENT

scale

measuring jug

melon baller

saucepan

fine-mesh sieve

airtight jar(s)

INGREDIENTS

200 g (7 oz) granulated white sugar

100 ml (3½ oz) water

100 ml (3½ oz) white-wine vinegar

handful fresh mint

1 tablespoon sea salt

2.5 cm (1 in) ginger

1 teaspoon chilli flakes (optional)

1 melon (honeydew, cantaloupe and watermelon all work, or you can use a mixture)

Try instead

Switch out the flavourings for different fruits and vegetables. Cucumbers can be pickled with dill and mustard seed for a more classic pickle, while stone fruits like peaches can be pickled with baking spices and lemon zest for a sweeter twist that works well with darker spirits.

Pairs well with

Vodka, contemporary gin, blanco tequila, lighter rum and mezcal.

METHOD

Combine the sugar, water, vinegar and mint in a saucepan and stir over a low heat until the sugar dissolves. Once it is about to boil, take it off the heat and allow it to steep for around an hour to infuse the mint. Strain and return the liquid to the saucepan. Add the salt, ginger and chilli and bring to the boil. Pack the melon balls into your jar as tightly as possible without squishing them. Carefully pour in the hot pickling liquid, making sure all the melon is covered and leaving about 1 cm (½ in) at the top of the jar. Seal and allow to cool. You can start to use these after a day or two, but the longer you leave them the more the flavour will develop.

STORE

When initially sealed, they can be kept in a cool, dark place for a week or so (longer if you jar them properly; see page 96). Once opened they should be stored in the fridge for up to 6 months. The melon will continue to soften though, so try to use them within a few months for a crunchier texture.

LACTO-NECTARINE SYRUP

Lacto-fermenting is a great way to preserve fruit at the height of its deliciousness. The sweet tanginess of nectarines works particularly well here.

PREP

Ferment the fruit ahead of time. Remove the stems and pits from the nectarines and roughly slice the fruit. Weigh your nectarines and calculate 2 per cent of the total weight – this is how much salt you will need – a golden ratio of salt to fruit which can work for lots of different recipes.

Try instead

This works for all manner of fruit. Chopped fruit will ferment more quickly than whole fruit, which can take up to a week or more.

Pairs well with

Honestly, anything! It is light and bright enough to work with lighter spirits, but has enough depth of flavour to stand up to heavier ones.

EQUIPMENT

scale
zip-lock bag
blender

INGREDIENTS

500 g (1 lb 2 oz) lacto-fermented nectarines
salt (see Prep)
250 g (9 oz) sugar (preferably raw sugar, but granulated white sugar is fine too)

METHOD

Combine the nectarine and salt in a zip-lock bag, squeezing to get rid of all the air before sealing it. Leave at room temperature in a dark place for 3 days (it is a good idea to pop it on a tray or in a tub in case of leakage). Monitor it daily – you should see the bag starting to expand. It should take around 3 days to fully expand, but obviously, if it looks like it's ready to explode then stop the fermentation earlier to avoid disaster! You can also let it go longer if there is no danger of it popping; a longer ferment will increase the depth of flavour. When it's ready, you should be able to taste an extra saltiness and acidity but nothing too funky or 'off'. There's no need to strain it, as everything in the bag can go in the final syrup.

Combine the nectarine and sugar in a blender and blend until smooth.

STORE

In an airtight container for up to 1 month.

MANGO AND JALAPEÑO HOT SAUCE

A fruity hot sauce is great to have in the cupboard to add a twist to Bloody Marys or Spicy Margaritas.

PREP

Peel the ginger and chop all the ingredients roughly. Make sure you check the chillies, and if any of the seeds/insides are discoloured (brown or black) cut those parts out – any healthy-looking seeds can stay in. Make your brine.

EQUIPMENT

measuring jug

saucepan

jar, preferably with an airlock/fermentation lid if you have one

strainer

blender

INGREDIENTS

500 ml (17 oz/2 cups) water

2 tablespoons salt

1 fresh or frozen mango, peeled and sliced

5 jalapeño peppers (see Notes)

5 cm (2 in) piece ginger

200 ml (7 oz) apple-cider vinegar, or to taste

1 teaspoon ground cumin (optional)

METHOD

Bring the water to the boil and add the salt, stirring to dissolve. Remove from the heat.

Pack your mango, chillies and ginger as tightly as you can into your jar. Pour in the brine so that everything is fully submerged. Try to leave as little space as possible at the top of the jar. Screw the lid on tightly. If you have an airlock lid, it will release pressure as it builds up. You can make this without one, just make sure to open the jar daily to release the built-up gas, trying to do it as quickly as possible to stop oxygen getting back into the jar.

Leave to ferment at room temperature away from direct sunlight for 3–7 days – the longer you ferment it for, the tangier it will be, but especially if you're not using an airlock it can be wise to err on the side of caution and stop the ferment sooner. Some cloudiness is to be expected but trust your senses – if anything looks or smells funky, best to chuck it and start again. Once you're happy with the ferment, strain it, reserving the brine. Add the solids and enough brine to loosen to your blender, along with some apple-cider vinegar to taste (I usually add this in smaller increments until it reaches a good acid balance) and the ground cumin, if using. Blend, and you're ready to bottle.

STORE

In a sealed container in the fridge for up to 1 month.

NOTES

I use jalapeño chillies as they are quite mild. You can absolutely switch them out for a hotter chilli like habanero if you want more of a kick, or mix a couple of different types of chilli in there.

TRY INSTEAD

Lots of different fruits make great hot sauces – I've had good success with passionfruit, or stone fruits such as peaches.

PAIRS WELL WITH

Vodka, lighter or heavier rums, blanco or aged tequilas and mezcal.

COCKTAIL
RECIPES

By now you should be prepped for success, so it's time to use the Flavour friends method (see page 45) to build the prep recipes into fully fledged, balanced drinks that hit all points of the Taste Triangle.

I find it much more useful to divide cocktails into moods; I hardly ever think 'I want a gin drink', but I do think, 'It's 3 pm, the sun is shining, I'm going to do a crossword in the garden and I want something refreshing and a bit lighter in alcohol so I can still cook dinner afterwards' or 'I'm stuffed after a big meal, give me something stiff and bitter to finish my night!'. So, this is how I have arranged the recipes here – based on situation and style. Every recipe can be used as a template for your own favourite spirits and flavours, so I have provided an example of this for each, and noted where a recipe is easy to make non-alcoholic.

I have also highlighted where a drink is particularly suited to a group serve, or any shortcuts you can take to make it easier to bash out a few at a time for when you're entertaining. The nice thing about these recipes is that while they take inspiration from classic cocktails, they're all 'original'. So, there's no wrong way to make them! Want to serve them in a different glass or with a different garnish? Go right ahead – I promise I won't be offended!

Tips and tricks for best results
+ Bear in mind that making home-made ingredients always takes a bit of trial and error – sometimes they'll come out a little sweeter, sometimes a little more bitter and so on. Trust your palate. There are few things a dash of sugar syrup, lemon juice or bitters can't fix.
+ Always use as much ice as you can. Ice insulates itself, so the more there is the longer it will stay cold and the more slowly it will melt. Try using decorative ice cubes; they look especially good in jugs for group serves.
+ Glassware should generally be chilled, especially if the drink is being served 'up' i.e. with no ice. The fridge is good, the freezer is better! If that's not possible, add a few cubes of ice to your glass and fill with water as you're building the drink, then tip it out when you're ready to pour the drink into the glass.
+ 'Single-straining' refers to using a Hawthorne strainer to hold the ice back in your strainer, but there will still be some small ice shards that make it through. I usually use this method if serving over ice as the small chips don't matter too much in that case. 'Double-straining' means using the Hawthorne strainer in the same way but also pouring through a fine-mesh sieve to remove all the shards of ice. I usually do this when serving drinks 'up'.

SERVICE

/ˈsəːvɪs/

noun

the work performed by one that serves;
contribution (of cocktails, in this case)
to the welfare of others

the action or process of serving food
and drinks to guests

LAZING ON A SUNNY AFTERNOON

These drinks are light, spritzy and refreshing. They're also generally pretty simple to throw together once you've done the prep, hence the 'lazy' part! I love this style of drink as a solo afternoon tipple instead of a beer, or as an easy welcome drink for a group event. You can even chuck the fixin's for some in a cooler and surprise your friends with something a bit fancier than a beer when hanging out in the park or at a beach*.

*Please check your local laws on drinking in these locations; I will not accept responsibility if any of you get arrested for drinking a Bellini in public.

BESPOKE BELLINI

As I mentioned in the recipe for the puree used here (see page 97), the Bellini format of puree and sparkling wine is ripe for switching up with seasonal fruit. The Bellini was invented at Harry's Bar in Venice, which I was lucky enough to visit a few years ago and had a great time. Their peach puree is literally just muddled peaches with very little sugar, so drinks more like peach juice. I prefer the texture from a bit more sugar, and tend to leave the blend a little chunky so you get bursts of fruit flesh through the drink – that counts as one of your five a day, right?

NOTE

You want a sparkling wine with quite high acid content, like a prosecco, otherwise you may need a small splash of lemon juice.

Group serve

This does fizz a lot as you are pouring the bubbles in, so if you are making a large quantity at once, mix it in a larger jug first and allow to settle before pouring into individual glasses.

Non-alcoholic option

This works really well with a dry ginger ale instead of the sparkling wine, or just soda water (club soda) if you prefer something less sweet.

Try instead

Switch this up seasonally. Some other combinations I've had good success with are strawberry and rosehip, honeydew melon and agave, or peach and lemon verbena.

EQUIPMENT

glassware: Champagne flute or wine glass

jigger (although this is one instance where I'll let you off with eyeballing; a healthy dollop or skoosh from a squeezy bottle is fine)

bar spoon

INGREDIENTS

45 ml (1½ oz) Pear and chamomile puree (page 97)

120 ml (4 oz) dry sparkling wine (see Note)

cubed ice

dehydrated pear, to garnish (optional)

METHOD

Add the puree to a glass and slowly pour in the sparkling wine. Stir to combine. Add ice (traditionally this drink doesn't have any, but sometimes I like to use a bigger glass and add some), then garnish with the pear, if using.

REBUJITO FRUTA

The Rebujito is, in my opinion, the ultimate summer refresher. Born in the Sherry Triangle in the south of Spain (where it gets HOT), they really understood the brief: the base is sherry, so low ABV and perfect for drinking all day in the sun, topped up with a lemon-lime soda. This take uses infused sherry to really punch up the juicy fruit factor, hence Rebujito fruta, or fruity Rebujito!

NOTE

You could try matching a flavoured syrup instead if you're feeling adventurous. Something like vanilla or raspberry and mint would work well here.

Group serve

You can pour these a little ahead of time with the strawberries in there and just add ice and a sprig as each guest arrives.

Non-alcoholic option

Make a strawberry and tarragon shrub (see page 86) and use that as the base instead.

Try instead

Change up the sherry infusion. Chamomile and ginger work well with salty manzanilla, or stone fruits and hardy herbs with a nutty amontillado. If you want to punch it up a bit, split the sherry fifty-fifty with a citrus-forward gin.

EQUIPMENT

glassware: highball
jigger
bar spoon

INGREDIENTS

60 ml (2 oz) Strawberry and tarragon fino sherry (page 105)

15 ml (½ oz) sugar syrup (see Note; see page 65)

30 ml (1 oz) lemon juice

soda water (club soda)

cubed ice

sliced strawberries and tarragon sprig, to garnish

METHOD

Add the sherry, sugar syrup and lemon juice to your glass and top with soda to just under halfway. Add ice and some strawberry slices, mixing so the slices are suspended in the drink. Garnish with a tarragon sprig.

SUNSHINE SPRITZES

What else says summer like a Spritz? The template of liqueur, sparkling wine and soda water (club soda) is infinitely adaptable. Here, I've given two different versions, one using a shrub and one using a ferment. These layer in flavour and interest to this simple drink to really elevate it.

Blueberry and lemongrass Spritz

EQUIPMENT

glassware: wine glass
jigger
bar spoon

INGREDIENTS

30 ml (1 oz) Blueberry and lemongrass shrub (page 89)

40 ml (1⅓ oz) amaro (anything red-fruited and citrusy will work well)

90 ml (3 oz) dry sparkling wine

30 ml (1 oz) soda water (club soda)

cubed ice

skewered blueberries left over from shrub and a mint sprig, to garnish

METHOD

Add everything to your wine glass with ice. Stir and garnish with the blueberries and a mint sprig.

Group serve

You can pour these a little ahead of time and just add ice and garnish as each guest arrives, or make up jugs.

Non-alcoholic option

Use a full 60 ml (2 oz) of the shrub or ferment and leave out the amaro. Replace the sparkling wine with tonic water (lemon tonic works really nicely here if you have it) to retain the bitter aspect, but still keep the splash of soda to lengthen it.

Try instead

The combinations of amaro and modifier are endless! You can do complementary or contrasting flavours. Try a citrus and delicate herb shrub with a juicy citrus amaro, or a berry and baking spice ferment with a more savoury amaro.

Lacto-nectarine Spritz

EQUIPMENT

glassware: wine glass
jigger
bar spoon

INGREDIENTS

50 ml (1¾ oz) Amaro Montenegro or other juicy, citrus-forward amaro

20 ml (⅔ oz) Lacto-nectarine syrup (page 130)

90 ml (3 oz) dry sparkling wine

30 ml (1 oz) soda water (club soda)

cubed ice

thyme sprig, to garnish

METHOD

Add everything to your wine glass with ice. Stir and garnish with a thyme sprig.

BOOZY ICED TEA

Every time I drink an iced tea I imagine I'm in a rocking chair on a wraparound verandah somewhere beautiful in the south of the United States, and that's a pretty nice image! Bourbon is the natural choice, but you can swap it for any other aged spirit. I love using tea in cocktails in general; it's a great way to add both flavour and dilution to drinks.

NOTES

*You can use whatever your favourite tea is. Mine is Scottish Breakfast, *wink wink*.*

The honey may need to be adjusted depending on how strong your tea is – dial it down for herbal teas, up for astringent black teas.

Group serve

This works really well as a jug serve too, just multiply the recipe and add ice to the jug if your guests all arrive together, or leave the jug un-iced and pour over ice in individual glasses.

Non-alcoholic option

Just leave out the bourbon!

Try instead

Switch out the tea and spirit. Try herbal teas, like lemongrass and ginger, with gin, or hibiscus with vodka, and amend the spices you use in the honey to match.

EQUIPMENT

glassware: highball (or tea mug!)

kettle or saucepan

jigger

bar spoon

INGREDIENTS

90 ml (3 oz) black tea (see Notes)

30 ml (1 oz) bourbon

20 ml (⅔ oz) Spiced honey or agave syrup (page 77; see Notes)

2 dashes Chilli tincture (page 120; optional)

splash soda water (club soda); optional

cubed ice

lemon wheels, to garnish

METHOD

Brew the tea of your choice according to the packet instructions, then leave to cool. Add everything to your glass with ice, then add a splash of soda water (if using) and garnish with lemon wheels. A couple of dashes of chilli tincture or other bitters is a fun addition to this flavour combination, but not necessary.

PUCKER UP

These are the drinks that make you sit up and take notice. Short, sharp and punchy, they make no apologies and take no prisoners with a full-on flavour profile and slurpable format. Who else has caught up with a friend for one Margarita and ended up having three? I can't be the only one! Forefronting the booze and fresh produce, I can't think of a better style of drink to properly kick off your night ... or end it.

SHERBET GIMLET

While modern Gimlets tend to use gin, lime juice and sugar, the original used just Rose's Lime Cordial and gin – a great example of using preserved ingredients to simplify the process! So, let's take that format and dial it up a bit. Using a home-made cordial means you have more control over the final drink, and can tailor it to other spirits. Tequila, for example, is a great match for the chilli spice here.

Group serve

This recipe works well as a batch as it is stable – just pour 90 ml (3 oz) total per drink and shake.

Non-alcoholic option

Use a non-alcoholic spirit, or just top up the sherbet with soda water (club soda) or ginger beer as a highball.

Try instead

This works with vodka, gin or lighter rum as well. Otherwise, mix up your sherbet – a warmer citrus like orange would go well with darker spirits.

EQUIPMENT

glassware: stemmed cocktail glass

jigger

shaker tins

strainers

INGREDIENTS

lime and chilli powder rim (if you feel like making that from the sherbet recipe on page 82, otherwise a dehydrated lime wheel or fresh lime wedge works too)

60 ml (2 oz) blanco tequila

30 ml (1 oz) Chilli lime sherbet (page 82)

2 dashes Mango and black tea bitters (page 119; optional)

cubed ice

METHOD

If rimming the glass, use a lime wedge to wet the edge of it and dip it into the chilli lime powder. Add the ingredients to your shaker tins with ice and shake hard. Double-strain into your glass.

FOGGY CALLING

This is a mashup of a London Calling and a London Fog with a twentieth century twist. What is it they say? There's no such thing as a new idea? Essentially, it's a short, citrus-forward gin drink that will put a pep in your step.

NOTES

London Dry or most contemporary gins work well here.

You can use an infused sherry, like strawberry, if you'd like to dial up the flavour even more.

Non-alcoholic option

Use a non-alcoholic spirit or shake up the syrup, lemon juice and bitters and add a spritz of soda water (club soda) to the glass.

Try instead

Blanco tequila or a lighter rum. You could also switch up the syrup or use a liqueur instead.

EQUIPMENT

glassware: stemmed cocktail glass

jigger

juicer

shaker tins

strainers

INGREDIENTS

50 ml (1¾ oz) gin (see Notes)

15 ml (½ oz) fino sherry (see Notes)

20 ml (⅔ oz) Vanilla and Earl Grey syrup (page 76)

20 ml (⅔ oz) lemon juice

2 dashes orange bitters (or make your own; see page 116)

cubed ice

lemon twist, to garnish

METHOD

Add all of the ingredients to your shaker tins with ice and shake hard. Double-strain into your glass and garnish with a lemon twist.

LADY MARMALADE

This is a late-night speciality in my household, using the jam made from our cumquat tree. Lady Marmalade always shows you a good time. Full of flavour, it is punchy and tangy. Additional garnish: karaoke.

Non-alcoholic option

Shaking up the marmalade and a tangy fruit juice like grapefruit with a splash of lime works well; the marmalade adds texture and complexity to elevate the juice into mocktail status.

Try instead

This works with aged tequila, brandy or whisky instead. You could also use a brighter marmalade based on lime, lemon or grapefruit, and switch the lime juice for lemon to pair with a lighter spirit. The Rhubarb and fennel jam on page 101 works well with gin and a berry liqueur for a different take. A dash or two of Mango and jalapeño hot sauce (see page 131) works really well in here as well if you're feeling spicy!

EQUIPMENT

glassware: rocks glass

jigger

shaker tins

INGREDIENTS

45 ml (1½ oz) mezcal

15 ml (½ oz) apricot brandy

2 tablespoons Spiced cumquat marmalade (page 100)

30 ml (1 oz) lime juice

cubed ice

cumquat halves, to garnish

METHOD

Add everything to your shaker tins with ice and shake hard. 'Dump' into your glass (i.e. don't strain, just pour in the same ice you shook with), adding more ice if necessary to fill the glass, then garnish with a cumquat half.

ANOTHER DAY, ANOTHER DAIQUIRI

The holy trinity of spirit, citrus and sweetener can be spun a thousand ways – a Daiquiri is just one example. Given that they're such simple drinks, the balance really matters here. There are two ratios I usually use: 2-parts spirit to 1-part citrus and ½-part sweetener gives a zingy and bracing drink, whereas 2-parts spirit to ¾-parts each citrus and sweetener softens it a little. Here I want the syrup at the forefront, and the tartness from the pomegranate in the grenadine balances it out.

Try instead

All sorts of spirits and syrups can be combined for infinite flavour combinations.

EQUIPMENT

glassware: stemmed cocktail glass

jigger

shaker tins

strainers

INGREDIENTS

60 ml (2 oz) lighter rum

20 ml (⅔ oz) lime juice

20 ml (⅔ oz) Hibiscus grenadine (page 71)

cubed ice

dehydrated lime wheel or lime wedge, to garnish

METHOD

Add all of the ingredients to your shaker tins with ice and shake hard. Double-strain into your glass and garnish with lime.

MELON MARTINI

While I love a dry or dirty Martini, this recipe is what I like to call a 'gateway Martini'. For this stroke of genius I have to credit John Hallett, head bartender at Goodwater, the bar I co-own in Melbourne with some friends. The fruity aspect helps take the edge off what is a very booze-forward drink, so try using it to convert any friends who aren't usually fans of a Martini!

NOTES

Using a lighter, contemporary-style gin will make this even more approachable, but London Dry works as well. You could also try another fruit brandy here instead of applejack.

Melon vermouth is simply dry vermouth infused with melon. Just take the offcuts from the pickled melon balls and sit them in vermouth overnight.

Group serve

This can be batched ahead of time and kept in the fridge or the freezer. You can even pre-dilute it. The easiest way to do this is to make one drink and calculate the difference in volume between the total ingredients and the final drink – that's the dilution, so just multiply that number by the amount of drinks you're making and add that amount of water to the batch.

Try instead

Mix up your pickles to suit the flavour profile of your gin. Pickled grapes are a fun option, too!

EQUIPMENT

glassware: stemmed cocktail glass

jigger

mixing glass

bar spoon

strainer

INGREDIENTS

50 ml (1¾ oz) gin (see Notes)

10 ml (¼ oz) applejack (see Notes)

25 ml (¾ oz) melon vermouth (see Notes)

2 bar spoons pickled melon brine (see page 127)

cubed ice

skewered Pickled melon balls (see page 127)

METHOD

Add all of the ingredients to your mixing glass with ice and stir until chilled and diluted. Strain into your glass and garnish with as many pickled melon balls as you like.

STAYCATION

While there's nothing quite like an actual vacation, mixing yourself up a fun and fruity drink at home is the next best thing! Cocktails are so transportive, and these recipes will whisk you away to tropical climes through fruit, spice and all things nice.

DEVIL'S ADVOCATE

Full credit for this one goes to my old colleague at Bomba, Ryan Casley. It is spicy, sweet and moreish. The original recipe used a spiced vanilla liqueur, but this interpretation leans on the combination of the Vanilla and Earl Grey syrup (page 76) with home-made bitters for a similar complexity.

Group serve

This works without the shaking – just build in a jug. Garnish with orange wheels (and some slices of chilli if you and your friends are hardcore).

Non-alcoholic option

Make an orange and chilli shrub (see page 86) instead of the vodka.

Try instead

The DIY spiced rum (page 107) works well here too, or gin. You can switch out the syrup for a spiced agave (page 77) instead.

EQUIPMENT

glassware: rocks glass

jigger

juicer

shaker tins

strainers

INGREDIENTS

Tajin rim, to garnish

50 ml (1¾ oz) Orange and chilli vodka (page 106)

20 ml (⅔ oz) Vanilla and Earl Grey syrup (page 76)

20 ml (⅔ oz) lemon juice

2 dashes Orange and coffee bitters (page 118)

cubed ice

100 ml (3½ oz) ginger beer

METHOD

Use a lime wedge to wet the edge of your glass and dip into the Tajin. Add all the ingredients except the ginger beer to a shaker tin with ice and shake hard. Single-strain into your glass, add ice and top with the ginger beer.

HOLIDAY HIGHBALL

The family of cocktails composed of a spirit, citrus, sweetener and lengthened with soda water (club soda) lends itself to infinite variations. Leaning into fruity flavours and serving on crushed ice (à la Mojito) means that it fits firmly in the holiday-mode category – also because it is very easy to make and nobody wants to work too hard on vacation!

NOTE

To crush your ice without an ice crusher, just wrap it in a clean tea towel (dish towel) and bash it up with something heavy like a mallet or rolling pin. If that's too much effort for your staycation, just shake and dump – this will break up the ice enough for a crushed effect.

Group serve
This works well as a jug serve.

Non-alcoholic option
Leave out the spirit and bump up the citrus and syrup. Using a splash of a flavoured soda, or ginger beer can help add more complexity.

Try instead
All sorts of spirits and syrups can be combined for infinite flavour combinations. The Hibiscus grenadine (page 71) could be matched with a light rum or gin, for example, or the Beetroot and apple cordial (page 74) with tequila. If you haven't had time to make a syrup, mix through some tinned passionfruit pulp for an extra pop of flavour.

EQUIPMENT

glassware: highball

jigger

juicer

bar spoon

INGREDIENTS

60 ml (2 oz) spirit of your choice (this works well with everything from vodka to tequila to whisky!)

20 ml (⅔ oz) lemon juice

20 ml (⅔ oz) Raspberry syrup with basil and mint (page 75)

crushed ice (see Note)

soda water (club soda), for topping up

mint or basil sprig, to garnish

METHOD

Add all of the ingredients except the soda water to your glass with ice and 'churn'. This will start dilution and should mean that your glass is quite full – often, too much soda is the main culprit in an underwhelming Mojito; it should really just be a splash at the end rather than a large part of the volume of the drink, and the same applies here. Top up with more ice if needed, then add a splash of soda and the garnish.

JUMPED-UP JUNGLE BIRD

The Jungle Bird is one of my favourite tropical drinks. It has all of the rum and pineapple you would expect from this style of drink, but Campari brings a bitter edge and interest. Here, we're using Coconut fat-washed Campari (page 110) to bring depth, and the Mandarin and pink pepper shrub (page 90) adds florals and spice for the best Jungle Bird you've ever had!

NOTES

You can absolutely use fresh pineapple juice but bottled works just fine, too.

Adjust the lime juice according to how sharp your shrub is; you may need a little more or a little less.

Group serve

This works well as a blended drink, more on the technique for that on page 186.

Non-alcoholic option

Shake up the pineapple juice with the shrub and add soda water (club soda) for a fun and frothy non-alcoholic option.

Try instead

This is quite a specific recipe, but the Coconut fat-washed Campari can be used in all types of tropical drinks for a bitter edge. Switching out the Mandarin and pink pepper shrub for the Banana skin oleo on page 83 can give a different spin.

EQUIPMENT

glassware: rocks glass
jigger
juicer
shaker tins
strainers

INGREDIENTS

45 ml (1½ oz) heavier rum

20 ml (⅔ oz) Coconut fat-washed Campari (page 110)

45 ml (1½ oz) pineapple juice (see Notes)

20 ml (⅔ oz) Mandarin and pink pepper shrub (page 90)

10 ml (¼ oz) lime juice (see Notes)

cubed ice

mandarin butterfly, to garnish (if you made them when making the shrub, otherwise a pineapple or orange wedge or a mint sprig)

METHOD

Add all of the ingredients to your shaker tins with ice and shake hard. Strain over fresh ice and garnish.

BALLER BATIDA

We all know and love a Piña Colada, but it doesn't have a monopoly on fruity, creamy cocktails. One of my other favourites is the Batida, a Brazilian drink. 'Batida' literally means 'shaken', and is quite a loosely defined combination of cachaça, fruit and lime, often with a creamy element of coconut milk or condensed milk. Cachaça is a sugar-cane spirit – essentially a Brazilian rum – so you can easily substitute it with another lighter-style rum instead.

NOTE

You can substitute the coconut milk for coconut cream or condensed milk – just use less as they are more intense than coconut milk.

Group serve

This works well as a blended drink (see page 186).

Non-alcoholic option

Just leave out the booze! You can increase the quantities of everything else to get a reasonable volume.

Try instead

All different fruits can work in this recipe – passionfruit syrup is a common one, but the Spiced cumquat marmalade on page 100 is delicious!

EQUIPMENT

glassware: rocks glass
jigger
juicer
shaker tins

INGREDIENTS

60 ml (2 oz) cachaça
30 ml (1 oz) Lacto-nectarine syrup (page 130)
30 ml (1 oz) coconut milk (see Note)
15 ml (½ oz) lime juice
cubed ice
lime wedge, to garnish

METHOD

Add all of the ingredients to your shaker tins with ice and shake. 'Dump' into your glass (or strain over fresh ice if you're feeling fancy!) and garnish.

A HARD
DAY'S NIGHT

Everyone needs a bit of luxury now and then, and these are the drinks to indulge with. Whether you like to cap off your evening with something boozy and rich, or prefer more of a dessert-style cocktail, I have you covered in this section. So, get dressed in your finest and spoil yourself!

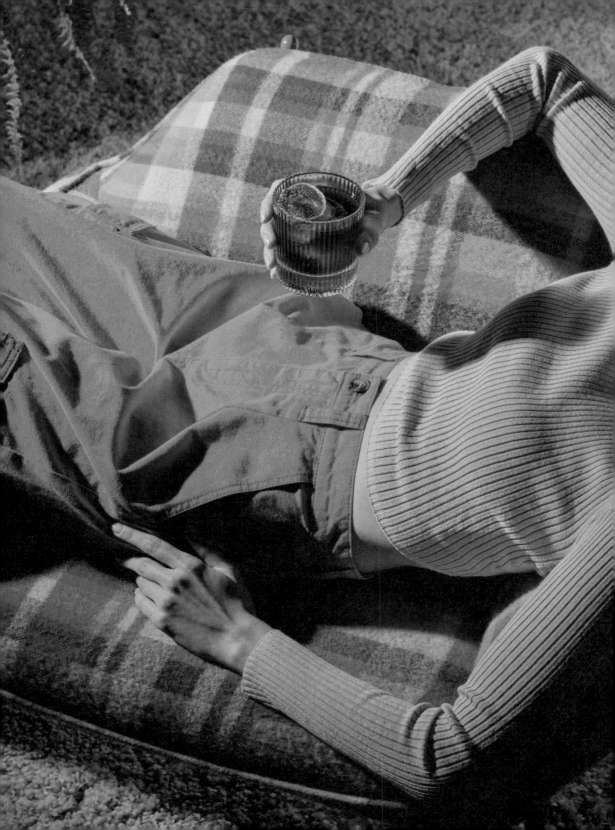

FIG OLD FASHIONED

The Old Fashioned's traditional format of spirit, sweetener and booze is a perfect template to mix and match with. Here, we lean into the rich flavour of the fig alongside a spicy rye whiskey, and the balsamic vinegar zings up the whole drink.

NOTE

Angostura is a good option, or you can make your own (see page 116).

Group serve

This can be batched ahead of time and kept in the fridge or freezer. You can even pre-dilute it. The easiest way to do this is to make one drink and calculate the difference in volume between the total ingredients and the final drink; that's the dilution, so just multiply that number by the amount of drinks you're making and add that much water to the batch.

Try instead

Lots of spirits and sweeteners can be combined here. Try using an aged tequila or mezcal with the Beetroot and apple cordial (page 74), the Vanilla and Earl Grey syrup (page 76) with bourbon, or the Banana skin oleo (page 83) with a heavier rum.

EQUIPMENT

glassware: rocks glass

jigger

mixing glass

bar spoon

strainer

INGREDIENTS

60 ml (2 oz) rye whiskey (bourbon or brandy work well here too)

15 ml (½ oz) Balsamic fig shrub (page 91)

3 dashes bitters (see Note)

block ice

fig from the shrub (if still pretty), or an orange twist, to garnish

METHOD

Add all of the ingredients to a mixing glass with ice and stir. Strain over fresh ice, preferably a large block, and garnish.

RHUBARB ALEXANDER

Rhubarb pie and ice cream is a belter of a dessert, so why wouldn't you want it in a cocktail?! The Alexander is a creamy nightcap, so this format works well. Gin was the original spirit used, although the Brandy Alexander is more well-known these days, and I'm using Scotch here. This recipe works well with all three, but the drink still lends itself to experimentation with different spirits and flavours.

NOTE

Something quite rich works here, and you want to steer clear of anything too heavily peated, although a little smokiness adds a nice edge.

Group serve

This works well as a blended drink – more on the technique for that below.

Non-alcoholic option

Leave out the spirit and add a splash of lemon juice.

Try instead

Blanco tequila and the Chilli lime sherbet (page 82) make an awesome boozy creamsicle, or go richer by using a darker spirit and a berry or stone-fruit syrup.

EQUIPMENT

glassware: stemmed cocktail glass

jigger

shaker tins

strainers

INGREDIENTS

45 ml (1½ oz) blended Scotch (see Note)

2 tablespoons Rhubarb and fennel jam (page 101)

30 ml (1 oz) cream or a scoop of vanilla ice cream

cubed ice

finely chopped fennel fronds or crushed fennel seeds, to garnish

METHOD

Add all of the ingredients to your shaker tins with ice and shake hard to make sure the cream is properly aerated. Double-strain into your glass and garnish with a light sprinkle of fennel.

VACATION NEGRONI

The perfect combination of strong, sweet and bitter, a richer-style Negroni makes an excellent digestif. This is inspired by the East India Negroni, invented by Jim Meehan of Please Don't Tell fame, but leans even further into the tropical notes of the rum using home-made ingredients.

NOTE

You could use a sweet vermouth instead of the sherry, but it is not as sweet as Pedro Ximénez, so you'd need to use a little more.

Group serve

This can be batched ahead of time and kept in the fridge or freezer. You can even pre-dilute it. The easiest way to do this is to make one drink and calculate the difference in volume between the total ingredients and the final drink – that's the dilution, so just multiply that number by the amount of drinks you're making and add that amount of water to the batch.

Try instead

Pair different spirits and amari with different home-made ingredients to keep this format fresh. Try a Boulevardier (American whiskey Negroni) with the Balsamic fig shrub (page 91), or a White Negroni (which uses Suze instead of Campari) with half bianco vermouth and half Strawberry and tarragon fino sherry (page 105).

EQUIPMENT

glassware: rocks glass
jigger
mixing glass
bar spoon
strainer

INGREDIENTS

45 ml (1½ oz) DIY spiced rum (page 107)

20 ml (⅔ oz) Coconut fat-washed Campari (page 110)

10 ml (¼ oz) Pedro Ximénez sherry (see Note)

10 ml (¼ oz) Mandarin and pink pepper shrub (page 90)

cubed and block ice

mandarin butterfly or orange twist, to garnish

METHOD

Add all of the ingredients to your mixing glass with cubed ice and stir. Strain over fresh ice, preferably a large block, and garnish with a mandarin butterfly or orange twist.

BEETS BY MEXICO

Stirred down drinks can still be fun, and here the Beetroot and apple cordial (page 74) adds a fruity and savoury edge to an essentially Manhattan-style drink. The mezcal adds an intriguing edge, which makes this drink very much an after-dark sipper.

NOTES

I like the nuttiness of the amontillado with the cordial, but you could use oloroso here instead for a richer drink, or stick to a sweet vermouth – I'd just use a little less to stop the overall drink being too sweet. Angostura bitters works here, or use something tailored to the flavour profile of the drink, but it definitely needs a kick of spice whichever way you go.

Group serve

This can be batched ahead of time and kept in the fridge or the freezer. You can even pre-dilute it. The easiest way to do this is to make one drink and calculate the difference in volume between the total ingredients and the final drink – that's the dilution, so just multiply that number by the amount of drinks you're making and add that amount of water to the batch.

Try instead

Simplify this by infusing the sherry itself (page 105). Stone fruit, orchard fruit, berries, baking spices and nuts all make great flavour combinations.

EQUIPMENT

glassware: stemmed cocktail glass or rocks glass

jigger

mixing glass

bar spoon

strainer

INGREDIENTS

45 ml (1½ oz) aged tequila

10 ml (¼ oz) mezcal

20 ml (⅔ oz) amontillado sherry (see Notes)

15 ml (½ oz) Beetroot and apple cordial (page 74)

2 dashes bitters (see Notes)

cubed and block ice

dehydrated apple slice or lemon twist, to garnish

METHOD

Add all of the ingredients to your mixing glass with ice and stir. Strain over fresh ice, preferably a large block, and garnish with an apple slice or lemon twist.

PARTY
STARTERS

While I've suggested options for group serves throughout the recipes, there are a couple of formats that just scream party, and that's punches and blended drinks! The main thing you want when hosting is to have a stress-free time, and punches and blended drinks are easy to prepare ahead of time and smash out while 'on service'. Punches are the original festive libation; they predate the first cocktails, but have stood the test of time as a well-balanced and amendable option that also looks great as a centrepiece. Blending, while it may have to be done in batches depending on the size of your group, is still easier than shaking or stirring – and the whiz of a blender always marks the start of a good time.

PARTY PUNCH

The classic punch proportion has a handy little rhyme to help you remember it: one of sour, two of sweet, three of strong and four of weak – catchy! The constituent parts of this can be anything you want. The sour usually comes from lemon or lime, but verjus can be a nice replacement. The sweet generally starts with an oleo (see page 78), which is built upon by liqueurs or syrups. The strong is spirits and fortified wines, and the weak is tea, water and/or soda water (club soda). Spices and other fruits double up as flavour enhancers and pretty garnishes. Decorative ice cubes look great as well.

This recipe makes about 10–15 serves depending on how generous your pour is, so just scale up or down from there!

NOTES

You can make the oleo in the bottom of your punch bowl ahead of time and simply stir to dissolve the sugar as you add other liquid. The lemon peel and thyme also work as garnish.

A liqueur would work as well in place of the grenadine – either orange or apricot would be my pick for this recipe.

Non-alcoholic option

You can leave out the booze and just use a combination of oleo, syrups or shrubs, fruit juices, teas and soda water (club soda) to make a delicious non-alcoholic punch.

Try instead

It's honestly hard to make a bad punch! As long as you taste for balance, let your creativity run wild.

EQUIPMENT

glassware: punch bowl or other large decorative bowl, serving glasses (punch bowls generally come with small glass tea cups, otherwise rocks glasses are fine)

measuring jug

scale

juicer

bar spoon

ladle

INGREDIENTS

400 ml (13½ oz) lemongrass and ginger tea

200 g (7 oz) Lemon and thyme oleo (page 81) (see Notes)

200 ml (7 oz) Hibiscus grenadine (page 71) (see Notes)

200 ml (7 oz) lemon juice

200 ml (7 oz) brandy

200 ml (7 oz) rye whiskey

200 ml (7 oz) oloroso sherry or semi-dry madeira

400 ml (13½ oz) ginger beer

4 cinnamon sticks

6 star anise

orange wheels and mint sprigs (or really anything pretty you have to hand), to garnish

cubed ice or decorative ice cubes

METHOD

Add the tea while still warm to the oleo and stir to dissolve the sugar. Add everything else to the bowl, including the garnishes. When ready to serve, add ice and ladle into individual glasses.

CLARIFIED COFFEE MILK PUNCH

As we've discussed, punches were popular far before refrigeration hit the scene, so enterprising hosts found another way to stabilise their signature serves – with milk-washing. It's a technique similar to fat-washing (see page 102) whereby you add milk to the mixture, which is acidic, causing it to curdle and clump (you can use citrus for this acid, or make an acid solution with citric or lactic acid). These 'curds' contain the perishable compounds, and so once they are strained out the drink becomes stable, and it can then be stored. Now that we *do* have fridges, I recommend keeping it in there! It can just be poured over ice to serve, making it great for parties. Again, you can use all manner of flavour combinations with a great result. Here, I've played into the dinner party idea and have done a coffee milk punch, which is a perfect way to wow your guests at the end of the night. This quantity should yield about ten serves depending on how much volume is removed in the curdling process.

NOTE

Alternative milks, like soy and coconut, can work here, but are a little trickier than regular milk to work with, so I recommend trying this with a dairy milk first to get the technique down before experimenting. You can flavour the milk – soaking some stale brioche or pastries in the milk for about an hour then straining before using would be delicious.

Try instead

You can clarify anything as long as you add the acid. Use the regular punch format above and just add milk! Using the Peanut butter bourbon in this (page 111) really kicks it up a notch!

EQUIPMENT

glassware: rocks glasses
2 large measuring jugs
juicer
fine-mesh sieve and either a coffee filter or muslin (cheesecloth)
bar spoon

INGREDIENTS

200 ml (7 oz) full-cream (whole) milk (see Note)
200 ml (7 oz) bourbon
200 ml (7 oz) oloroso sherry
200 ml (7 oz) cold-filter coffee
80 ml (2½ oz) Spiced honey or agave syrup (page 77)
30 ml (1 oz) lemon juice or lactic acid solution (see page 27)
block ice
orange twist or grated dark chocolate (or both!), to garnish

METHOD

Have the milk ready in one jug and add everything else, except the ice, to another jug. Slowly pour the punch mixture into the milk, stirring gently – you should see it start to curdle. Gently move the curds around to encourage them to clump together. Leave to split, about 10 minutes, and then pour gently through your chosen filter. The resultant liquid should be clear and delicious! To serve, keep chilled, pour directly over a large ice block into the glass and garnish.

BLENDED BEBIDA

There are a few key things to bear in mind with blended drinks.
Try to have everything cold when it goes into the blender; dropping
room-temperature ingredients on ice will just cause it to melt and
you'll be left with a runny drink. About 250 g (1 cup) of ice per drink
is good. Because the cold numbs your flavour receptors, you can
pump up the sweetness more than you usually would in a drink,
otherwise they taste thin. You also want to keep an eye on how
much booze is in there because of alcohol's lower freezing point;
too much and it won't freeze. Here I have used Pear and chamomile
puree (page 97), but any puree or frozen fruit can be used to flavour
all manner of spirits. If using fresh fruit, chop it and stick it in the
freezer for a few hours before using. I have done this recipe per
drink, but you can scale it up with as much as will fit in your blender.

NOTE
*Orange liqueur would work
as well as sugar syrup here,
but you will need to decrease
the tequila to 45 ml (1½ oz)
to lower the booze.*

Non-alcoholic option
Use a fruit juice like grapefruit or
watermelon in place of the spirit.

Try instead
Most classic cocktail recipes
can be adapted for the blender
by adding more of the sweet
components.

EQUIPMENT
glassware: large stemmed
cocktail glass – and a wide straw
helps as well

jigger

juicer

blender

INGREDIENTS
60 ml (2 oz) blanco tequila

30 ml (1 oz) Pear and chamomile
puree (page 97)

15 ml (½ oz) sugar syrup
(see Note; see page 65)

30 ml (1 oz) lime juice

250 g (1 cup) ice

dehydrated pear, to garnish

METHOD
Working as quickly as possible, add all of your chilled ingredients
to the blender with ice. Start blending slowly then go to full
speed. As soon as all the ice is blended, stop. Otherwise, you
may overheat your drink. Pour into your glass and garnish with
dehydrated pear.

AFTERWORD

Thank you for accompanying me on this journey of flavour; I hope I've sparked some inspiration for you to get creative yourself. As with all things in life, practice makes perfect. Mastering the techniques in this book puts a world of flavour combinations at your fingertips for you and your guests to enjoy. So, now you know!

ACKNOWLEDGEMENTS

First of all, thank you to everyone who has watched and commented on my videos and articles. Hearing your questions has helped me reimagine how I approach drinks making, and how to keep it fun and exciting for those who don't have a bar's worth of booze to play with. It was this that inspired the book, and you guys are my inspiration for continuing to write about and create drinks and cocktails.

Thank you to all of my friends and family who have supported and encouraged me through the writing process. Special thanks to my fiancé Fred for keeping me fed, watered and reasonably sane, and my crews at Goodwater and Bomba for covering my absences and listening to me whinge. To the wider hospitality community, thank you for your endless creativity and expertise, especially Jacob Taylor and Kayla Saito for helping me with certain sections of this book.

The team at Hardie Grant are always a pleasure to work with – thank you Simon Davis for liking the idea to begin with, Ana Jacobsen and Andrea O'Connor for whipping the book into shape, and the design team; Celia Mance, Gareth Sobey and Melinda King for making it beautiful.

INDEX

Published in 2025 by Hardie Grant Books, an imprint of Hardie Grant Publishing

Hardie Grant Books (Melbourne)
Wurundjeri Country
Level 11, 36 Wellington Street
Collingwood, Victoria 3066

Hardie Grant Books (North America)
2912 Telegraph Ave
Berkeley, California 94705

hardiegrant.com/books

Hardie Grant acknowledges the Traditional Owners of the Country on which we work, the Wurundjeri People of the Kulin Nation and the Gadigal People of the Eora Nation, and recognises their continuing connection to the land, waters and culture. We pay our respects to their Elders past and present.

This book uses 250 ml (8½ fl oz) cup measurements and 15 ml (½ fl oz) tablespoons.
In the US, a cup is 8 fl oz (240 ml), just smaller; American cooks should be generous in their cup measurements; in the UK, a cup is 9½ fl oz (284 ml); British cooks should be scant in their cup measurements.
Imperial liquid measurement conversions are given just as 'oz', not 'fl oz'.

 A catalogue record for this book is available from the National Library of Australia

NATIONAL LIBRARY OF AUSTRALIA

Behind the Home Bar
ISBN 978 1 76145 080 8
ISBN 978 1 76145 081 5 (ebook)

10 9 8 7 6 5 4 3 2 1

Publisher: Simon Davis
Head of Editorial: Jasmin Chua
Project Editor: Ana Jacobsen
Editor: Andrea O'Connor
Creative Director: Kristin Thomas
Designer: Celia Mance
Photographer: Gareth Sobey
Stylist: Melinda King
Head of Production: Todd Rechner
Production Controller: Jessica Harvie

Colour reproduction by Splitting Image Colour Studio
Printed in China by Leo Paper Products LTD.

MIX
Paper | Supporting
responsible forestry
FSC® C020056

The paper this book is printed on is from FSC®-certified forests and other sources. FSC® promotes environmentally responsible, socially beneficial and economically viable management of the world's forests.